5 Cs &
BEYOND
Differential Approach to Credit

I0479874

PUNEET NAGPAL

INDIA · SINGAPORE · MALAYSIA

Notion Press

No.8, 3rd Cross Street,
CIT Colony, Mylapore,
Chennai, Tamil Nadu – 600004

First Published by Notion Press 2020
Copyright © Puneet Nagpal 2020
All Rights Reserved.

ISBN 978-1-64919-966-9

Dedication

With The blessings of the Almighty, I dedicate this book to—

My parents Mr. D.R. Nagpal and Mrs. Darshan Nagpal whose blessings have always guided me towards success in life.

My wife Rakhi, who is always by my side and gives me the strength to handle tough situations with ease. Her motivation has made it possible for me to write this book.

My lovely kids Saranshi and Shreshtha, whose smiles have always been my inspiration to do new things in life.

Contents

Foreword

"5Cs & BEYOND" is a unique book authored by Puneet which speaks of the practical facets of credit and its applications. The author's excellent communication skills and lucid writing power have made this book very interesting, and hence a must-read for all in the fraternity.

– Ashish Agarwal
Global Head Wholesale Banking – Yes Bank Ltd

"5Cs & BEYOND" – an idea conceived and scripted by Puneet Nagpal has resulted in his maiden masterpiece. I have personally worked with Puneet and watched his silent, smiling personality. He exudes an "aura" of being totally involved and gives his 100% with passion and integrity. The brilliance of this book is in its innovation of coming out and presenting the boring part of the job with finesse and simplicity. He combines his personal experience and lives, each moment of the process, through live experiences. His maiden effort through this book covers the basics of credit with rationale and a live perspective. There is no doubt that whoever picks up and reads this book will immensely benefit and significantly improve her/his credit skills.

– Neeraj Dhawan
Chief Risk Officer – Yes Bank Ltd

"5Cs & BEYOND" is a practitioner's book of credit assessment of a small and medium businesses in India. Puneet has a keen insight, grounded business understanding, a rare credit sense, and a rarer common sense, that makes this book so worthy. Each case reveals patterns of information which, when put together with personal discussion, financials, and market information, leaves one with pearls of wisdom. This book would jumpstart many a career in understanding credit to small and medium businesses, and build curiosity for learning through the case studies. Kudos to Puneet.

– Dr. (PhD) Malcolm Athaide

Co-Founder and CEO – Agrim Housing Finance

"I cannot recall a book that amalgamates the theory and practice of credit underwriting so deftly. It is lucid, focused and brings alive the real-life situations that credit professionals face in their daily experience. This book will be a useful guide to any practicing credit professional."

– Ambrish Sharma

Zonal Head, Credit Risk (Retired), ICICI Bank

Preface

The five C's of credit stand for Character, Capacity, Capital, Collateral and Condition. This framework helps to evaluate the creditworthiness of a potential borrower and predicting the probability of default. As a credit manager, all of us use this framework to analyze the credit. These five principals have become an integral part of our credit analysis and have become the base of our evaluation process.

Through this book, I have tried to touch upon traits of credits which are extensions of the 5C's and also those concepts which have a direct and indirect correlation with the credit domain. They are equally important in maintaining good underwriting as well as monitoring standards. These are those aspects of credit which play vital roles in creating a differential between a good and average credit practice and introduce the credit manager to a broader picture and purpose than rather holding him or her up to the stage of initial underwriting only.

In terms of the core credit concept, I have added the 6th "C", namely **Compliance,** which is remarkably important for financial institutions and the credit managers associated with them. With some of the developments in the last 1-2 years in the Indian financial domain, knowledge and understanding of the 6th C has become very important and hence, I thought it relevant to make it part of this book

I have also tried to touch upon the behavioural and managerial aspects which, though do not fall under credit tool categories, are equally important for a good credit practice. These are skills which come with the experience of going through various situations faced by the credit manager.

This book is not a step by step approach to credit but it provides guidelines for credit managers to take a rational credit decision, ensuring a healthy portfolio. We shall not be talking about available credit tools and their applications but about the basic approach for good credit underwriting, decision making and monitoring. There are tools and there are skill sets—the right mix and use of these leads to good credit decisions. Tools are those we have studied about from the books during our college time; skill sets are acquired through continuous learning and the flair to learn from the experiences of others as well.

Effort has been made to move from the static concept of one-time credit analytics to the dynamic concept of ongoing credit analytics during the complete life cycle of the customer relationship.

All the above-mentioned discussions are distributed across eight chapters starting with **Chapter I** which discusses understanding the business of the company on which we are going to have a credit exposure. It talks about the requirement for a holistic approach to be an integral part of our credit decisions. All the parameters, whether internal to an entity or related to external business environment, are to be considered. This chapter introduces readers to concepts like the *'Five Minute-Connect Strategy'* and *'Parallel Line' Model.*

Understanding the business of a client is the foremost requirement for good underwriting. However, equally important is to structure the credit through the types of transactions which can be carried out on the basis of the strength of the business and the available mitigants. This is what **Chapter II** talks about. This approach is equally applicable to standalone case underwriting as well as placing a structure around granular cases where we need to have an analytics-based approval approach. This chapter introduces the *'Business-Transaction Matrix'* to the readers.

Chapter III talks about phase through which the business is passing and our credit strategy for that phase. It introduces the reader to the *'Inflection Curve'* approach to identify the position of the business at the time of taking exposure or review of entity. It also introduces readers to *"Tunnel Concept"*, which talks about support systems availability in form of cash flows and net worth in funding of a project.

One very important facet of credit underwriting is understanding the character of the person on whom we are taking a credit exposure. There are many *dedupe* sites which help in gaining an idea about the promoters through their past credit history. Additionally, there are informal sources of reference about promoters which provide information directly from the horse's mouth. I have introduced the concept of **'MORE'** with respect to market reference in **Chapter IV** which throws light on the importance of market referencing, KYC and *dedupes*.

The above-mentioned four chapters talk about the assessment of credit strength of an entity as well as the character and capacity of its promoters to take a credit exposure. For a credit and business analyst, this is a job half done. What is important is to keep the underwritten accounts and portfolio in good health during their lifecycles. This warrants for strong post-disbursement monitoring of both the individual account as well as the portfolio. **Chapter V** is about the monitoring of the portfolio and will take you through the flowcharts on the monitoring process which are named as **'The Skeleton of Monitoring'** and the **'Pyramid Approach'**.

As I say that Compliance is the 6th "C" of credit, I have dedicated **Chapter VI** to compliance and internal controls. Most of the time, we think of compliance as a regulatory or organizational process requirement and that is where we undermine this area and leave scope for breach of defined processes. The chapter defines '**Compliance Goal Keepers**' and insists on developing a culture of compliance.

The financial sector is transforming fast with respect to digitization and automation. Automation, digital and analytics are replacing mechanized operations in banks, thus leading to better banking experiences for customers and improvement in the productivity of an organization. In **Chapter VII,** I have not explained the present digital applications as I know every one of us is well aware of them. What I have tried to explain is the thought process to be developed in ourself and same to be deployed in our daily working so as to make ourself future ready. The chapter is knitted around the concepts of **Adaptability, Learning and Design Thinking.**

I have concluded the discussion with **Chapter VIII,** which talks about the soft skills required for a Credit Analyst. There are many personality traits which could have been mentioned here but I have captured four of the traits which, I feel, need to be necessarily a part of the personality of a credit analyst. Understanding our subject and job requirements is a basic requirement and most of us understand this. However, these are the traits which make her or him stand apart from others.

I have provided pages at the end of the book for noting down points which you may feel valid and important and also for noting down points where you may require clarity. And above all, I will request you to jot down suggestions for me to work upon while penning down future works. I am available on my email ID: puneetnagpal368@gmail.com/puneetnagpal368@hotmail.com

Acknowledgement

I would like to express my sincere gratitude to my seniors and colleagues for guiding, mentoring and supporting me. Special thanks to Mr. Parag Gorakshakar and Mr. Mahavir Agrawal for giving their valuable suggestions which I incorporated in my book. I also acknowledge the support of my team in providing me with feedback from time to time on practical situations they encountered on the field. These feedbacks have been great enablers for writing this book. I also recognize the blessings, love and psychological support provided by my elders, relatives and friends. This has provided me with the ever-required warmth in my journey till now.

Lastly, special credits to my HR and Media team in giving me a 'go-ahead' for publishing this book.

Chapter 1

Understanding Business

On the warm afternoon of June in some place of Maharashtra, my team and other banker members in multiple banking were sitting in the meeting room with our customer. The customer was doing a presentation along with his team. He was trying to justify the requirement of additional funds from the banks despite a fall in the sales of the company. The company could not achieve previous year estimates plus its sales in the first 2 months of the present year were low on a year-on-year basis.

The customer was into manufacturing of heavy engineering products which were a major part of EPC projects in the Oil and Gas sector and the major customers were MNCs and Indian corporates. The customer's business dealings with these principals were fairly long, with an average period of 6-7 years and had received regular repeat orders from them over the years.

As the discussion progressed, the customer explained the reason for the non-achievement of the estimates submitted to the bank. There was deferment of order pick-up by one of his big buyers as a result of the overall delay in the project for which this engineered equipment was part of. The pickup was rescheduled for Q2 of that year. This was the reason for low sales and led to funds getting trapped into work in progress stocks. In the meantime, one of his regular customers had put an order for express delivery of some parts. This was a catch twenty-two situation for the client and was the precise reason for an urgent meeting with the bankers. The client was in dire need of additional funds.

Once the customer and team were done with their presentation, we asked them to give us half an hour to have a discussion between all the bankers on the funding proposition. There was a long silence in the room after the customer and team left. There were all-natural apprehensions in everyone's mind about the credit exposure on the company as total banking exposure as on that date was 1.2x of the turnover. This was really a precarious situation wherein the company could not achieve the projections basis which we enhanced limits last year. Additionally, first 2 months of the present year were quite dismal.

We had a long discussion with everyone and the meeting concluded with other bankers turning down the request of the client and decided to keep account under close watch. We were now left in a dilemma of whether to go ahead with funding or should we go ahead on the same line as other bankers.

What was holding my team and me from saying "No" was the 3 years of satisfactory track of client with us, high energy and enthusiasm of promoter, regular plough back of profits by the promoter in the company to take care of growth and strong capital base. Additionally, the company had shown regular growth in all the previous years except past year.

We decided to have a second round of discussion with the client and team and revisited order details, purchase ledgers, despatches, stock audits to validate his claims, which we could do. Post this, we went through the production floor to see ongoing activity. *We could observe synchronization between what we saw on the floor, the client's version and the disclosure from the records.*

Based on the above, we took the decision to go ahead and provide short term funds for execution of orders in hand. It was quite heartening to see that in the next six months, the client could deliver the old orders plus new orders in hand which enabled him to have additional orders placed by buyers due to his abidance to timelines. In another 3 months, the promoters shifted all the salary accounts plus their individual accounts to our bank along with additional limits from us.

Above is an example of taking an informed decision after understanding the business well. We could have easily said "No" for providing required support if we have not understood the requirement of the business. Declining or rejecting cases is quite easy but taking the above decision requires a balanced approach on the part of an analyst.

Understanding the business model of the entity on whom we are taking a credit call is the first and foremost requirement for good analysis. A good way is to use Porter's Five Force Model to analyze the industry of customer on the five parameters of Competition level, Suppliers bargaining power, Buyers bargaining power, Entry barriers and Competition intensity.

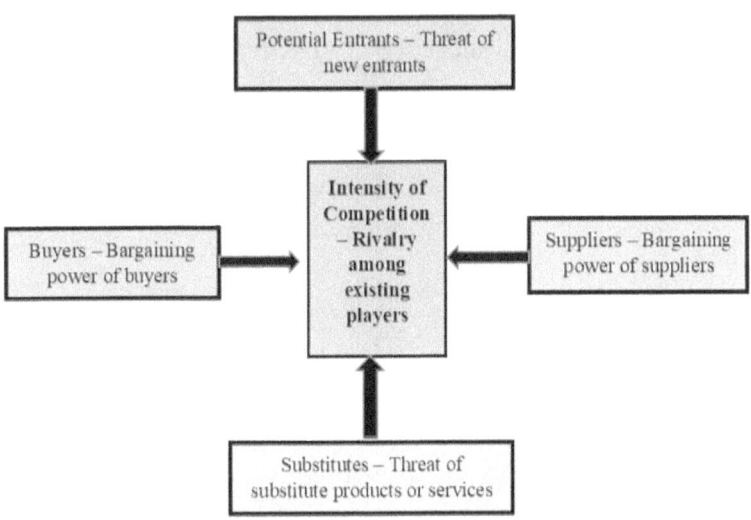

Porter Five Force Model

These insights about the industry provide understanding about the strong and weak areas in the business model of the company. On the individual company front also it is very important to have an idea about the position of the client in the whole Supply Chain. This enables us to predict the company's business movement in correlation with the overall industry.

Different industries have differential financial profiles (Financial Ratios) and business cycles (Working capital cycles). Within a particular industry, different businesses have differentiated financial profiles and business cycles. Further, within a particular business domain, manufacturers, traders or service providers will have different financial profiles and business cycles.

Let us understand this point through diagrammatic representation (Venn diagram):

- Rectangle (the outer one) here represents the universe of industries

- Red (R), Blue (B) & Green (G) represents the universe of Pharma, Auto and Textile industries

- R1 and R2 represent API and Formulation industries respectively; B1 and B2 represent passenger vehicle and commercial vehicle industries respectively; G1 and G2 represent Yarn and Readymade industries respectively

- Within each sub-industry, there are three rectangular Venn diagrams (Activity wise) representing manufacturers, traders and service segment

- Intersections within sub-industry segments and activity segments represent similarity in financial profile and business cycles as some players undertake manufacturing, trading and services concurrently

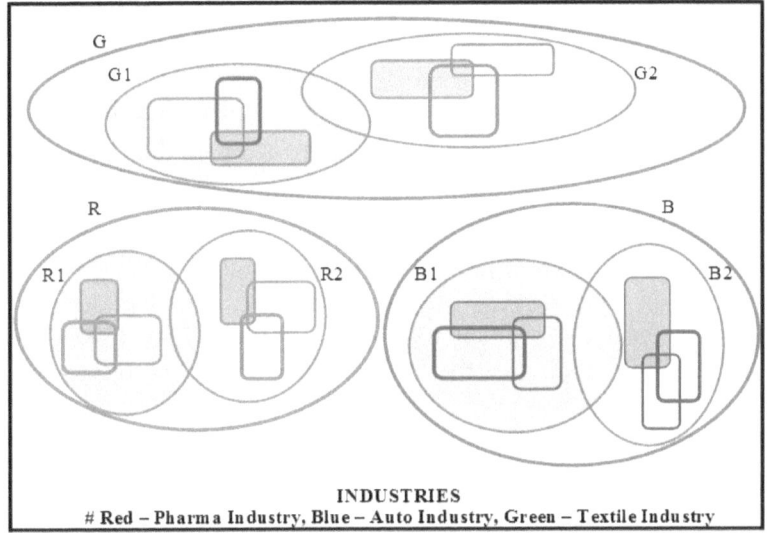

INDUSTRIES
Red – Pharma Industry, Blue – Auto Industry, Green – Textile Industry

Similarly, seasonality also plays a role in differential business cycles. Entities engaged in agricultural activities will have a seasonal procurement cycle and yearlong sale while on other side exporters of garments to European and American nations will have yearlong procurement and production with major sales near Christmas season. Similarly, Schools or any educational institutes will have high creditors in the balance sheet with very low current ratio. Largely, business cycles for some of the industries may fall in the following zones:

Table: Sales/Working Capital (times) for selective industries

Healthcare	Automotive	Communications	Hospitality
Metals	Technology	Retail	Packaging
Aerospace	Chemicals	Engineering	Pharma

Top Row – Higher than average; Middle Row – Near to Average, & Bottom Row – Lower than average

Note: It is indicative and varies from time to time according to the demand cycle through which particular industry is passing

It is also pertinent to understand the complete Supply Chain end to end for an entity. The requirement of funding will vary according to the placement within the Supply Chain. Retailers, wholesalers and manufacturers will have different cycles and different financial profiles within the same industry.

Overall, our approach in analyzing the business of an entity must be stepwise mapping in the following fashion so as to have the right benchmarking:

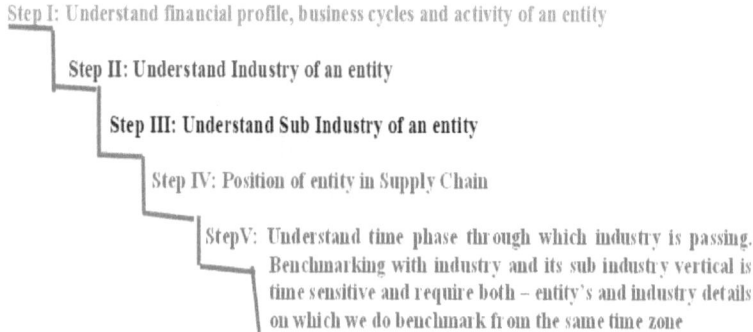

Step I: Understand financial profile, business cycles and activity of an entity

Step II: Understand Industry of an entity

Step III: Understand Sub Industry of an entity

Step IV: Position of entity in Supply Chain

StepV: Understand time phase through which industry is passing. Benchmarking with industry and its sub industry vertical is time sensitive and require both – entity's and industry details on which we do benchmark from the same time zone

Will take your through three scenarios, which surely will bring clarity to above discussion point:

Scenario 1: Financials of Company ABC (Value in Crores)

Parameter/Year	201x	201y	201z
Sales	100	110	120
Margins	10%	12%	15%
Capital	10	20	30
WC Debt	15	20	25

Total Debt (WC + Term Loans)	25	29	33
Creditors (days)	60	50	70
Gross Working Capital (WC) (value)	25	30	35
Fixed Assets (P&M)	10	9	8

Facts available from B/s and P&L:	Industry Fact Check:
✎ Sales *increasing* consistently + Margins *improving* consistently + Capital *improving* year on year ✎ WC Debt *increase* on year on year + WC also *increasing* consistently ✎ Sales to WC (times) – Average of 3.5 ✎ Sales to FA ratio – Average of 12.5 WC Debt to Sales is increasing, however still in a satisfactory range of 20%	✎ *Positive* as on date. Seeing *growth* due to demand ✎ Average margins of 12% ✎ Average Sales to WC is 4 times ✎ Average Sales to FA ratio of 12

Conclusion:

✍ Company is doing the *same as industry* in terms of sales

✍ Company is doing *better than the industry* in terms of margins

✍ Company is showing *consistent improvement* on sales and margins

✍ In terms of operating efficiency company is an *average player* with Sales to WC and Sales to FA (P&M) comparable to the industry *average* only

As a prudent analyst, with above credentials, we can go ahead for taking exposure on this client

Scenario 2: Financials of Company XYZ (Value in Crores)

Parameter/Year	201x	201y	201z
Sales	100	110	120
Margins	10%	10%	10%
Capital	10	12	15
WC Debt	15	25	40
Total Debt (WC + Term Loans)	25	34	46
Creditors (days)	60	50	70
Gross Working Capital (WC)	25	35	55
Fixed Assets (P&M)	10	9	8

Facts available from B/s and P&L:

- Sales increasing consistently + Margins maintained on year on year + Capital improving year on year
- WC Debt increase on a year on year+ WC also increasing consistently
- Sales to WC (times) – Average of 3
- Sales to FA ratio of 12.5
- WC Debt to Sales ratio is deteriorating and is high at 33%

Industry Fact Check:

- *Positive* as on date. Seeing *growth* due to demand
- Average margins of 12%
- Average Sales to WC is 5 times
- Average Sales to FA ratio of 12

Conclusion:

- Company is doing the *same as the industry* in terms of sales
- Company is *not doing good* in margins as compared to industry
- Company is showing *consistent improvement* on sales and has been able to *hold on to margins*
- In terms of working capital management, the player is *inferior to the average player* and the *cycles seem to be strained*

> ✍ Seems client has adopted *strategy of push sales to compete* with other players and hence is providing *long credits* in the market. This has led to a higher-than-average requirement of WC debt which going forward may affect margins also. This strategy carries a *high risk* as default by some buyers going forward can put a big amount at risk which may wipe out all past gains
>
> **As a prudent analyst, with the above credentials, we may avoid the exposure on this client**

Scenario 3: Financials of Company PQR (Value in Crores)

Parameter/Year	201x	201y	201z
Sales	100	95	97
Margins	10%	10%	10%
Capital	10	15	20
WC Debt	15	14	14
Total Debt (WC + Term Loans)	20	17	14
Creditors (days)	60	50	70
Gross Working Capital (WC)	25	24	20
Fixed Assets (P&M)	10	9	8

Facts available from B/s and P&L:	Industry Fact Check:
✍ Sales *more and so stagnant* on year on year + Margins *maintained* on year on year + Capital *improving* year on year	✍ Average as on date. *Stagnant* in last 2 years due to low demand
✍ WC Debt *decrease* on year on year + WC also *decreasing* consistently	✍ Average margins of 8%
✍ Sales to WC (times) – Average of 4	✍ Average Sales to WC is 3 times
✍ Sales to FA ratio of 11	✍ Average Sales to FA ratio of 12
✍ Sales to WC debt *constant*	

> **Conclusion:**
>
> ✍ Company is doing the *same as the industry* in terms of sales
>
> ✍ Company is doing *better than the industry* in terms of margins and is able to maintain same
>
> ✍ In terms of working capital management company is *better than the industry*
>
> ✍ Seems client has adopted strategy of *selective sales* so as to keep *margins intact* and *low WC cycles.* Management will *wait for the right time* to accelerate sales
>
> **As a prudent analyst, with above credentials we can go ahead with exposure on this client**

Sometimes, financials of an entity are remarkably good vis a vis industry. Looking to the financials on *standalone*, all of us will surely give decision in affirmation only. However, deeper insight into numbers, business models and transactions in bank along with benchmarking with similar players in the industry may reveal a different story. We can comprehend the same from one of the incidents I am providing here:

CASE: Bank ABC received a proposal wherein the entity XYZ was into trading of metal and tin sheets. XYZ has shown a decent growth of 15-20% over the years in turnover and in last one year it has recorded 100% growth in sales. Additionally, financials of XYZ were quite good with low gearing, low leverage and shorter working capital cycle compared to other players in the industry. Overall, financials and the operations were relatively much better than other players in the market. According to the promoters, entity could do 100% growth in turnover post opening branch in *new geography*. Conduct of the account with the existing banker and also reference checks from all the buyers and sellers from the *existing geography* were also satisfactory and hence there was no reason for bank to turn down the requested enhancement through takeover of the account.

Despite all the parameters being quite satisfactory and better than industry, one thing which continually bothered banker was – *"How can this entity do so good" and especially in last one year it has achieved 100% growth in business from new geography when all the players in the same geography have stagnant sales.* Banker decided to do further digging in the account and hence took reference check of XYZ and the its top 3 buyers from the new geography. To the surprise of a banker, nobody from the *new geography* was aware about the customer and its 3 top buyers. On further deep dive and additional referencing, banker could find that there was cartelization between these players and the transactions between them were meant to be with the purpose of keeping sales ticking.

Now, the question arises—Does analysing financial profile and business cycles and benchmarking same with industry provide complete insight into business of an entity. Answer is "No." Two activities which need to be carried along with all the analysis are –

1. Meeting key management personal to ascertain the reasons for entity performing different from other players of the same industry. Personal meeting can also throw light on genuinity of financial numbers

2. References from the market, which we shall discuss in detail in chapter 4.

Meeting with the promoters of an entity is important part of overall sanction process and there is a way to do so. I call this a **"Five Minute Connect Strategy"** wherein we start our conversation with letting client to speak about himself and his business, family background, successors, aspirations, vision, market conditions i.e. for initial 5-10 minutes it has to be monologue wherein client speaks and we listen. We shall keep our query points post listening to a person on the other side of the table. Discussion in this fashion will provide us a good insight into the model of the business, entity's standing in the market vis a vis competitors, customers and suppliers. *During the course of discussion, we shall observe that not only most of our questions are answered but we also gain new insights about the business, industry, market, geography etc.*

In fact, in case of manufacturer, prefer to meet client at its manufacturing facility so as to have better idea of complete production process. We may have observed that sometimes entities engaged in same business have different profit margins. The answer lies in the efficiency levels achieved by an entity due to better integration of backward and forward activities.

As already discussed in previous section, financials provide details on working capital management and opportunity to benchmark with the industry averages. What is important is to see balance sheet figures plus statements plus rating sheets (all three) in integration with downloads from meeting with customer. *Meeting and talking to management help in corroboration of facts analyzed through initial scan of financials and rating sheets and it can be other way round also wherein we can validate the version put up by a client during the discussion by going through available information in hand.* It also helps to remove ambiguity on points where we require further clarification.

CASE: Let me share one of my experience in respect of the customer whose proposal was received on my table and after going through the financials of entity I was quite apprehensive in funding to it. Reason for this was very high margins compared to other industry players. Client was into supplying of engineering goods to some government organization and its profit margins were nearly 1.5x to 2x of other players in the same segment. I decided to meet the client to understand the business and the reasons for exceptionally good profitability. I met the client at their manufacturing facility and what I observed after going through the unit and downloads from discussion was:

1. **Fully integrated unit** starting from designing to fabrication, wire drawing, electrical panelling to painting and then the finished product. Client has complete fabrication unit consisting of laser cutting machine and advanced welding equipment. Additionally, it also owned complete paint shop along with ovens

2. **Well segregated sub-units** for manufacturing of different products within the manufacturing facility. Client maintain separate books to ascertain unit wise profitability so as to have efficiency at sub-unit level

3. **Manufacturing and supply** of complete kit for a particular product along with installation service and after sales services. No other player in the industry was supplying a complete kit

In addition to the above distinction in manufacturing setup, what I observed in promoters were:

1. Their **involvement in end to end process** to control costing of products. Both the promoters were fully engaged from bidding of contracts to final delivery and after sales thus ensuring full satisfaction for the buyer

2. Their **involvement in designing the products**. Both the promoters were engineer and use to design the products on their own. Since, both of them were also engaged in manufacturing process, they use to save good percentage of wastage in overall manufacturing process

3. Their **engagement with employees**. Average service vintage of employees was 10 years. Overall work environment was quite conducive for employees

After returning to my office, the first thing I did was to sign the proposal. This customer proved to be one of our best assets in the portfolio. If I would not have visited the client's facility and discussed with him, I would have ended up with declining the proposal considering financials to be too good to believe.

Many a times during my interaction with client I have heard them saying that substantial part of their time goes into taking care of banking operations. Some of the observations made by them are listed here. I feel that our right understanding of client's business can also take care of these common grievances which in turn will lead to better client-banker relationships:

    a.   Non adequate credit facilities vis a vis business requirement

    b.   Delay in sanction of adhoc limits

    c.   Sanction of regular incremental facilities not in time of requirement

    d.   Long turnaround time in funding term loans for capital expenditure

    e.   Tenors and usance of import or export facilities not in line with overall business cycle

Consider a scenario by placing ourself in place of customer facing all the above issues. We surely will be doing some or all of the following:

    a.   Will lose our precious time in running after banker rather than doing business

    b.   Will miss opportunity to grab additional orders

    c.   Will have to continue with stagnant sales due to delayed capital expenditure

   d. Will likely face overdue in the account as a result of short drawing power, as actual working capital cycle is longer than what is accepted by the bank

   e. Will lead to lower hygiene scores thus lowering chances of additional funding

   f. Will think of shifting business from the bank

Understanding business of client also enable us to pitch right products to the customer and also let us structure funding right as per the requirement. Many a times, some business-like agriculture/ export etc. require peak level credit facilities to take care of their fund requirements at the time of procurement. Hence if we have understood the requirement of client well, we can provide peak and non-peak credit facilities to the client which shall ensure seamless operations for the client and also will make monitoring of account easy. In some of the businesses where client's business is majorly order backed, requirement of additional funds arises on receipt of bigger orders than that in normal course of business. In this scenario, client require additional credit facilities on urgent basis, which can be provided as a pre-approved adhoc credit facility to be used once or twice in a year for a particular tenor. This shall ensure smooth business for client and will lead to have strong bonding between banker and customer.

So, after going through above daily life situations, we have understood that how important is to understand the business of the client. On this line I am giving you a simple model which I have always followed while analyzing the proposal and have named it as **"Parallel Line Model."** Under this model you can draw two parallel number lines depicting intrinsic and extrinsic factors which can have major influence on the business of an entity.

Parallel Line Model

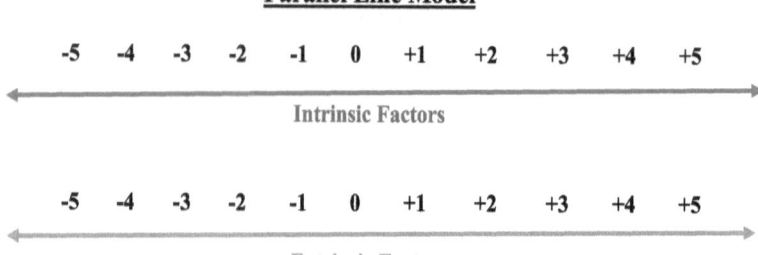

Both the lines are calibrated up to +5 on positive side and up to -5 on negative side signifying rating scales range from -5 to +5

Now plot your identified intrinsic and extrinsic factors individually on this number line with maximum marks of +5 and minimum of -5. I normally take following 4 factors under intrinsic and 3 factors under extrinsic category. You can alter number of factors by adding additional parameter relevant to particular time phase but would recommend to keep at least these 7 factors intact to have reasonable understanding of the business.

Four important intrinsic factors influencing business are:

1. Management quality – Vintage, net worth, vision, education basis discussion and downloads from client at the time of meeting

2. Vintage of business – Number of cycles through which business has gone through

3. Financial Strength – Leverage, Liquidity, profitability and also includes past repayment trend

4. Sustainability and Continuity of business – Succession plans, growth strategy, expansion plans

Three important extrinsic factors influencing business are:

1. Industry of operations – Outlook on the industry. Whether it is positive, neutral or negative. Phase through which it is passing. Check it on Porter 5 force model.

2. Position of client in supply chain – Strategic importance of client in overall supply chain

3. Overall economic condition of the country at particular point of time and expected trend going forward

Let us take the Case mentioned above to understand the analytic part of the model:

Intrinsic Factors:

Factor	Marks	Rational
Management Quality	+5	High vintage of promoters with good net worth and education in the area of operations with full involvement
Vintage of business	+5	Long vintage of an entity for more than 20 years in same business
Financial Strength	+4	Exceptional margins with leverage less than 1 and current ratio of 1.5 and above. Only adverse point was working capital cycles higher than average in the industry. However, looking to financial strength of balance sheet we deduct only 1 point from +5
Sustainability and Continuity of business	+5	Regular growth of business in past along with good order position which is 2x of last year turnover. Both the generations are already in the business and 3rd was getting ready to join business in next 2-3 years

Extrinsic Factors:

Factor	Marks	Rational
Industry of Operations	+4	Client was supplying to central government corporate with regular orders however there was some delay in payment of vendors but not too long. With government push on the particular segment, outlook was positive
Position in Supply Chain	+3	As explained, client was providing complete kit of a particular product to the principal along with after sales service and hence its position was quite strong in overall supply chain. 2 marks deducted from +5 looking to its medium size of operations
Economic Condition	+2	Slowdown in overall economy was evident however government was increasing spending to accelerate the growth and hence 2 points

Once, we have assigned score to all the factors, sum of all comes to Twenty-Eight (28) which is 80% Score (Score is calculated by dividing 28 to 35, which is sum total of maximum marks). **Further, this 80% implies cumulative score of +4 marks (80% of +5) on positive line, which is quite good score and hence we can consider this business to be quite strong. Normally, any business with cumulative score of 50% (≥ +2.5) and above can be considered as strong business model, 0 to less than 50% (≥ 0 & <+2.5) is average while anything <0 is weak model**

In my career journey as a banker, I have observed that the best learning school is customer's office and its manufacturing facility and the best learning session is interaction with client across the table. With this we are closing this chapter and will see going forward in next chapter that how this become important part in overall decisioning of case.

Chapter 2

Nail it Right

(Understanding Business and Transaction together)

When we receive any loan proposal for decision, what all we see through? Do we look to the business alone? Or we look to the transaction to be undertaken in isolation? Or we take decision basis mitigants in form of collaterals or defined credit structures only? Considering any of the dimension alone for decisioning shall not be a rational approach. We require to have a comprehensive evaluation of a proposal on all the above three dimensions. Missing on any one of these may lead to a weak credit with vulnerability to adverse movement in business environment.

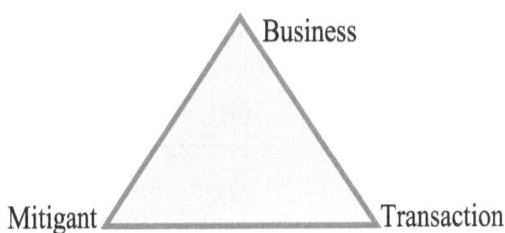

Business, as explained in earlier chapter, is a function of Intrinsic and Extrinsic factors linked to an entity.

Transaction, an operational side of relationship is defined by the form of credit lines that can be sanctioned to the client.

Mitigant, is either collateral or covenant that ensure full or partial recovery of funds in case asset turns delinquent.

Following table introduce all the three dimensions in brief:

Business	Transaction	Mitigants
Intrinsic and Extrinsic Factors as explained in Chapter I	1. Self-liquidating credit facilities 2. Project specific funding 3. Short term funding 4. Contingent Facilities 5. Secured Credit Facilities 6. Unsecured Credit Facilities 7. Export and Import limits and so on	1. Immovable properties 2. Cash securities 3. Escrow arrangements 4. Corporate guarantees 5. Personal Guarantees 6. Govt. Guarantee Schemes like CGTMSE, ECGC etc 7. Any other covenant strengthening credit

It is pertinent and significant to analyze business of entity, transactions to be approved and available mitigants or covenants to be put, after evaluating all the major risks associated with the proposal.

Every proposal carries with it different kinds of risks under domains of both financial risk and non-financial risk, all leading to credit loss for a lender if not taken care or plugged. Risk is inherent to all the lending activity we do and we cannot eliminate it. However, through right approach to appraisal we can reduce it in order to have optimal Risk-Return mix. As a prudent lender while considering a proposal we have to give due consideration to:

✓ different risks associated with the proposal

✓ degree to which the identified risks can adversely affect our exposure

✓ ways and means to contain these risks

Let us have a small refresher on some of the major risks associated with lending activity:

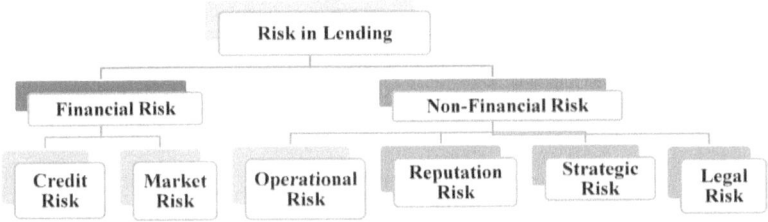

There are other risks also associated with lending however largely all of them can be categorized under Credit Risk, Market Risk and Operational Risk:

- ✓ **Credit Risk:** It is the risk of a default on a debt that may arise from a borrower failing to make required payments. It can be a:

    A. Counterparty Risk/Default risk or,

    B. Concentration risk or,

    C. Country risk

- ✓ **Operational Risk:** It is the risk of loss resulting from inadequate or failed internal processes, people, and systems, or from external events. It can be a:

    A. Internal and external fraud risk or,

    B. Process and Policies non adherence risk or,

    C. Risks arising from natural calamity events

- ✓ **Market Risk:** It is the risk of loss originating from adverse movement of market. It is a systematic risk and cannot be eliminated through diversification, but can be hedged. It can be a:

A. Interest rate risk or,

B. Currency rate risk or,

C. Commodity price risk

As a lender our step wise approach towards any proposal can be as:

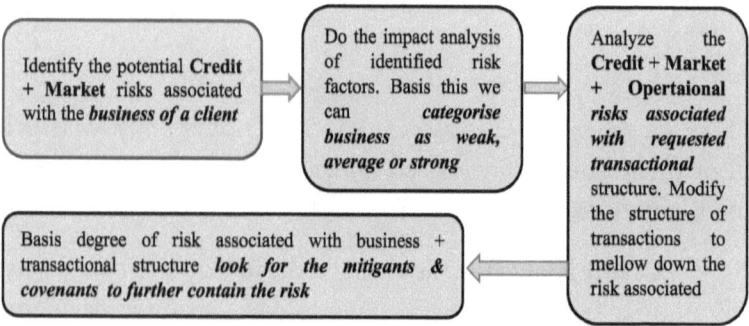

We will take our discussion ahead with a following matrix, which I call *"Business-Transaction Matrix"*:

Business-Transaction Matrix

B		Transaction		
		High Risk	**Medium Risk**	**Low Risk**
u s i	**Weak**	1	2	3
n e	**Average**	4	5	6
s s	**Strong**	7	8	9

#Business of client is plotted on Y axis and transaction on X axis

@There are nine scenarios depicting combination of business strength and risk profile of transaction

Matrix imparts objectivity and ensures uniformity in our underwriting basis different scenarios captured in it. For assessing business strength, we shall use the "Parallel Line Model" (explained in chapter-I) which rate business from Weak to Strong basis Credit Risk and Market Risk associated with business. While the Intrinsic factors carries Credit Risk, Extrinsic factors have both Credit Risk and Market Risk (for example – Commodity risk which can affect whole industry).

Once, *we have rated business*, we shall *rate the transaction credit lines* as requested by the client or transactional credit lines with existing bankers in case of takeover. Transactional Credit Lines are evaluated for high, medium or low risk *on standalone basis without any reference to business and available mitigants*. We can take help of following quadrant analysis:

Operational Risk - Market Risk Quadrants

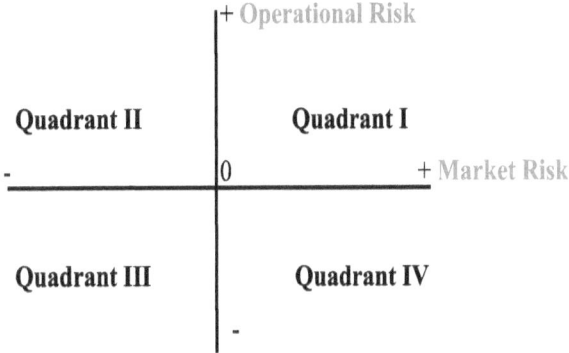

Note: + implies lesser risk and – implies higher risk

We shall provide higher weightage to Market Risk than Operational Risk at transactional levels. Operational risk is related more to lapses and non-adherence of processes, systems and policies (considering, fraud risk being largely taken care through initial screening before login of the proposal by separate risk division like Risk Containment Unit). Keeping this thought as foundation:

- *Quadrant I (QI) will qualify for Low Risk Transaction*

- *Quadrant IV (QIV) for Medium Risk Transaction*

- *Quadrant II (QII) & Quadrant III (QIII) for high risk Transaction*

Post categorizing operational and market risk in different quadrants, we can rate transaction credit lines as High Risk, Medium Risk or Low Risk transaction in following fashion:

Credit Risk associated with transaction	Quadrant classification for Operational and Market risk associated with transaction	Overall Risk Rating of Transaction
High	QI/QII/QIII/QIV	High Risk
Medium	QII/QIII	High Risk
Medium	QI/QIV	Medium Risk
Low	QII/QIII	High Risk
Low	QIV	Medium Risk
Low	QI	Low Risk

Let us consider following examples to explain the concept of transaction risk:

Example 1: Company ABC is sanctioned import LC limits of Rs. 50 Cr by a bank. Client put up a request for issuance of single import LC of Rs. 30 Cr. Company imports plastic granules for sale in local market. This is a time when there is high volatility in oil prices with rupee showing gradual slide against dollar.

Considering a profile of transaction, we can see that:

1. Credit Risk is High as it is quite a big transaction vis a vis sanctioned limit. Hence, it carries high devolvement risk

2. Market risk is High as it carries both adverse commodity price risk as well as adverse currency movement risk. We can reduce Market Risk to some extent by providing forwards to client, still Market risk shall be high as plastic granule trading business is being done at very low margin and if there is no end to end selling tie-up, it can lead to loss on the transaction

3. Operational Risk can be considered Low here considering transaction-based limit, and exposure being taken on regular asset-based customer whose KYC has already been done at the time of onboarding.

Hence, it shall lie in Quadrant II and Credit Risk as High. Hence, overall Transaction risk is "High"

Example 2: Company XYZ is sanctioned import LC limits of Rs. 50 Cr by a bank, against Fixed Deposits. Client put up a request for issuance of single import LC of Rs. 30 Cr. Company imports plastic granules for sale in local market. This is a time when there is high volatility in oil prices with rupee showing gradual slide against dollar. Client provided mark-up in form of FD to cover forex fluctuation. LC tenor is 90 days.

In this transaction our:

1. Credit Risk is "Nil"

2. Market Risk is "Low" as client has provided mark-up in form of additional FD to take care of normal forex fluctuation

3. Operational Risk is "Low." Client is not an asset customer for a bank and in case of some statutory demand in future during currency of our exposure may lead to bank interest in jeopardy. Hence it can be termed as Medium as a transaction is quite big and bank fall back is on FD only. However, it is a short tenor transaction and hence we can categorize same as "Low" Risk

It shall lie in Quadrant I and hence overall Transaction Risk is "Low"

Example 3: Company PQR, which is into EPC business, is sanctioned Bank Guarantee limits of Rs 100 Cr by a bank, against Fixed Deposits. Client put up a request for issuance of single Bank Guarantee of Rs 50 Cr in favour of some Indian government institution. Bank Guarantee is to be issued for 5 years

Transaction has:

1. Credit Risk as "Nil"

2. Market Risk as "Nil"

3. Operational Risk as "High." Though, it is 100% FD backed transaction, bank is entering into a very long tenor BG contract. Taking such a long-term call implies high uncertainty for a bank in terms of future statutory position of client and execution risk which may lead to extension of BGs beyond 5 years of initial terms

It shall lie in Quadrant IV and hence overall Transaction Risk is "Medium"

Further, I feel that after going through the matrix and the discussions above, it is natural to have some queries in mind which I would like to answer here:

Question A: Can we move the business from Weak to Average or Average to Strong?

Answer: "No." This attribute is related to factors beyond our control. This is the way the promoters carry their business and we have no say in it.

Question B: Can we move transaction from High Risk to Medium Risk or Medium Risk to Low Risk or directly from High Risk to Low Risk?

Answer: "Yes." With modification in type and structure of credit facilities, transaction can graduate from High Risk to Low Risk. This can be done by:

a. Replacing higher credit risk facilities with lower credit risk facilities which have higher Product Recovery Rate (PRR) (ex: Partial replacement of Cash Credit Limits with Invoice discounting limits, high usance LCs with shorter usance facilities, restricting financial BGs to some percentage of total exposure etc)

b. Hedging credit lines susceptible to market movements

c. Sanctioning self-liquidating credit lines like post shipment and bill discounting

Question C: Does all high-risk transactions need to be moved to medium or lower risk category?

Answer: Not necessarily. Transactions need to be viewed in combination with business and in cases where the business is rated strong, we can go ahead with suitable mitigants.

Question D: Whether all scenarios stand chance of funding with available mitigants? Can we take a decision of funding in different scenarios **basis available mitigants?** If yes, then up to what extent we would like to cover our risk. In other words, **up to what extent we can keep our exposure unsecured?**

Answer: Let us understand this Scenario wise

Scenario 1: Business – Weak and Transaction – High Risk

Avoid it, as the likelihood of credit going bad is very high. There are exceptions – Say A is an entity which is a start-up and we have a corporate guarantee of holding or group entity B, whose business falls in Strong category and has the capability to take care of entity A in case A defaults. In fact, in all the scenarios where the entity has support from group entity in the form of corporate guarantee, we should rate the business of corporate guarantor also.

Scenario 2: Business – Weak and Transaction – Medium Risk

Avoid. This is also a very fragile proposition from credit risk perspective except where it is backed by strong cash flows of the parent entity as explained under Scenario 1

Scenario 3: Business – Weak and Transaction – Low Risk

May be considered with strong transaction structure and very good security. Example for this scenario is – Let there be a standalone entity with low vintage and falling under the weak business category. However, the entity is in a niche segment supplying or providing services to all the established large corporates. Looking to this profile, there is an opportunity to fund with low-risk transactional structures like bill discounting thus shifting our exposure from entity to corporates. Additionally, we may take security to take care of any adverse situation.

Scenario 4: Business – Average and Transaction – High Risk

It is a situation where our borrower may have moderate vintage with modest financial strength and falling under lower bands of investment-grade rating. However, the nature of transactional structure requested may be high risk which increases the risk of the overall proposal. Under this circumstance, our approach should be to move the transaction from the high-risk category to medium risk category so that overall risk shall lie under Scenario 5. This scenario will require very strong mitigant, in case we decide to take credit exposure.

Scenario 5: Business – Average and Transaction – Medium Risk

This scenario will require relatively moderate mitigants than that required under Scenario 4

Scenario 6: Business – Average and Transaction – Low Risk

This scenario will require relatively moderate mitigants than that required under Scenario 5

Scenario 7: Business – Strong and Transaction – High Risk

Scenario 8: Business – Strong and Transaction – Medium Risk

Scenario 9: Business – Strong and Transaction – Low Risk

These three scenarios indicate quite strong fundamentals of an entity which normally suggests mid to high band of investment-grade rating for it. These are the entities who have the capability to rebound back in case some transactions do not go the intended way. They also have strong repayment tracks. So, the difference between these three scenarios will be of taking mitigants with highest in scenario 7 to lowest in scenario 9.

CASE: Entity XYZ was into trading of mobiles from the last 20 years. The entity was one of the big distributors for the top brands in the industry. Any new company launching its products in the Indian market used to connect with it for taking their distributorship. Since XYZ was enjoying this privileged treatment, it hopped from one principal to another and could command better margins than it used to have from earlier ones. In fact, in a decade it changed more than 6 principals.

As a result of exponential growth in business, the entity's requirement of funds was increasing. Bank provided it all the timely support in the form of Financial Bank Guarantees and Letter of Credits. On one occasion, XYZ approached the bank for incremental credit exposure, which was considerably high. The sanctioning authority asked the credit analyst to meet client and understand its strategy going forward on the business, fund arrangements and banking arrangement as the bank had already taken quite high exposure.

During the meeting, it was observed that client had a business growth plan, which was quite aggressive:

1. The client was looking for 3-4x growth in the top-line without evaluating its own financial capability to support this growth. Promoters were relying too much on debt from the banks

2. Promoters were looking for launching their own brand of feature phones along with the present business of distributorship without a well-thought distribution strategy

3. Though the entity's business was growing by leap and bounds, its business model does not seem to be stable. The promoter was changing principals frequently

4. The industry also carries high product obsolescence risk due to introduction of new product every alternate day, and such an aggressive stance could prove counterproductive in future

Overall, the client was drifting from average business profile to weak business profile in light of very fast growth pace vis-a-vis resources available to support the growth

In terms of Business-Transaction Matrix, it can be explained as under:

> The client was in **Scenario 5** with **Average Business and Medium Risk Transaction**. Bank's exposure was in the form of LC with lower transaction risk plus Financial BGs with medium transaction risk. LC has higher Product Recovery Rate (PRR) while Financial BG has zero PRR. Hence, it can be termed as Medium Transactional Risk

 Migrating to

> Now the client is drifting towards **Scenario 2 with Weak Business and Medium Risk Transaction**

After submission of call report, sanctioning authority declined enhancement and took the decision to gradually reduce bank's exposure and exit relationship. As a short-term measure, the bank strengthened its security structure to mitigate the high risk envisaged after hearing to the customer. Bank provided XYZ with adhoc for the immediate transaction under execution so as not to put immediate brakes on the business. In turn, the bank took quite strong collateral to strengthen their overall security structure.

CASE: I will now take you through another situation to deepen our understanding on this Matrix. Bank A received a proposition to fund an entity PQR which was:

- In the business of trading speciality chemical for the last 3-4 years.

- Its profit margins were in line with the industry and there was regular growth in the top line. Leverage was higher than the industry average

- Product was 100% petroleum derivative and used to be imported by limited big players in the industry who then use to sell it to the smaller players like an entity PQR. Entity PQR use to take supplies from one of the biggest suppliers and supply it to two to three MNC clients in the country

- Annual supply rates were fixed with customers but purchase rates with suppliers were fixed on a quarterly basis

- Entity was availing normal cash credit facilities from the existing banker

- Proposition received by the bank A was to fund cash credit which was well secured by good-quality collateral

Financials of an Entity (Value in Crores)

Parameters/Financials	201x	201y	201z
Sales	100	115	135
EBIDTA (%)	5.2%	5.5%	5.3%
Capital	8	10	12

WC Debt	20	23	25
Term Debt	8	7	9
Gearing (Ratio)	3.5	3	2.9
Current Ratio	1.4	1.4	1.4

Let us analyze the situation on Business-Transaction Matrix:

> Business

  1. Vintage – Low

  2. Financials – Moderate

  3. Supplier Concentration/Bargaining Power – Very High/Very Low

  4. Customer Concentration/Bargaining Power – High/ Low

  5. Industry – Susceptible to fluctuation in crude

Overall, this was a Weak Business

> Transaction – Normal cash credit facilities – High PRR facility. **Overall, this was a Medium Risk transaction**

This combination fits in Scenario 2 of our Matrix and as we already explained, it is a very fragile proposition from a credit-risk perspective. Hence, the bank proposed the customer with the following Business and Transaction structure to move the overall deal towards Scenario 5, i.e. Average Business with Medium Risk Transaction:

  1. Bank proposed that the customer freeze purchase leg prices on an annual basis to mitigate raw material price fluctuation risk. However, the client refused to do so as its bargaining power with the supplier was very limited.

2. Bank further proposed that the customer have its bill discounting facilities instead of plain vanilla cash credit facilities as bill discounting facility has lower PRR than cash credit limits. By doing so, the bank could have shifted credit risk from entity PQR to corporates who were its buyers. However, the client did not agree to that also.

Basis disagreement on the above points, bank A turned down the proposal

Existing banker of an entity enhanced the limits on the comfort of additional collateral. Everything was fine with the client, probably for next 7-8 months, till the time there was considerable upward revision in prices of chemical by the supplier. For the period in reference, there was upward revision in prices of the commodity plus adverse movement in currency. Since, entity PQR had annual contract at fixed price with the buyers, it started incurring losses due to higher purchase price vis a vis sale price. Company's requests to buyer and seller for price revision were turned down. The customer stopped supplies to customer leading his business to come to a halt and also led to non-repayment of old payments by the buyer on the pretext of breach of contract. This led to account turning NPA.

Business-Transaction Matrix is a dynamic concept. Out of three dimensions, Business is a "Time Variable" dimension and can move in any direction with time while other two dimensions – Transactions and mitigants are governable. Business can move either in a positive direction from Weak to Average to Strong Business or it can become weak over time and drift from Strong to Average to Weak Business. Hence, it is fairly important to have regular watch on the matrix movement of the account. In case of a **rating downgrade** of the account (not the facility), we need to review the account for corrective action. Another scenario which makes a case for review of the matrix for the account is overall movement in Industry. Any adverse movement in industry fundamentals will surely affect an individual entity and hence may lead to a shift in the position of account in the matrix. Similarly, any upgrade in credit rating and positive movement for an industry may lead to shift of account towards lower-risk area and can provide an opportunity to take higher risk.

Chapter 3

Time it Right

I commented in a previous chapter that Business is a dynamic concept, which means that business may or may not be same during the different phases of time to come. Also, the strategy with which the business has been run till date may or may not be suited for the business in the future.

Have observed that sometimes we commit the mistake of viewing account in a narrow context. We give disproportionate weightage to the past conduct and performance or available external credit rating of the account for taking a decision. Yes, past track or rating of an entity are strong indicators of performance and they always will have good weightage in overall decision-making. However, looking at a proposal from these dimensions only and negating other factors may not be the correct strategy. In fact, the credit rating of an entity will always come with a lag as there will always be a gap of doing the due diligence of account and release of rating by an agency. Over this, if we are referring the rating which has been provided 4-5 months back will certainly lead to a gap in understanding the present position of the account.

Important is to have a comprehensive analysis based on both past trend and the anticipated future path of an entity. We need to ask ourselves **"Are we entering into a relationship at the right time."** Though this statement seems to be simple but in real life, this requires understanding and analysis of several factors – internal as well as external to an entity. It implies that we need to superimpose future picture over the past performance. Let us seek the answer through Time Axis and Inflection point analysis:

See the following diagram:

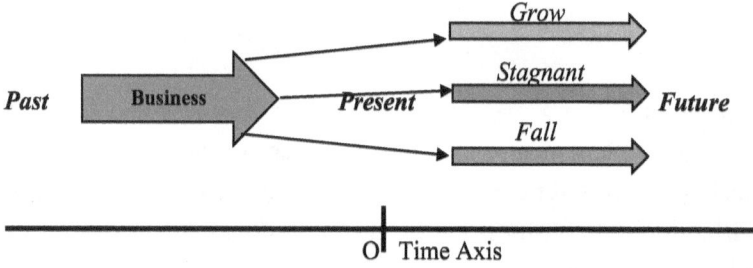

Let at point O (Present day) of Time Axis, we receive a proposition which is either of following:

- An existing asset customer with proposition for regular review

- An existing asset customer with proposition for incremental exposure

- A new to bank asset relationship

Now let's see the following graph in relation to Time Axis:

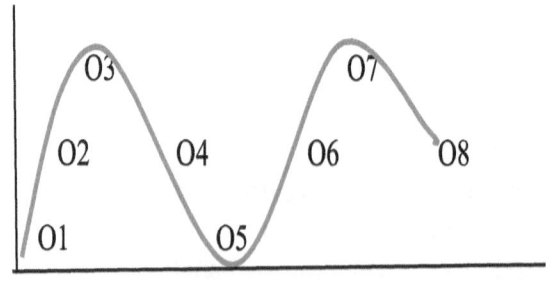

Inflection Point Curve (IP Curve)

Graph provides the various stages through which the entity has passed and may pass through in the future. Points O1 to O8 provide the probable position of a business at present (shown as point O on Time axis). The curve depicts various phases of growth, fall and stagnancy of Time Axis. Let us elaborate to have understanding of the curve:

- Point O1 indicates a start-up entity in the high-risk phase. Good point for venture capitalists to invest in the business

- Point O5 indicates an entity on death bed with low probability of revival

- Point O2 indicates an entity in its growth phase depicting good investment phase

- Point O6 indicates an entity with good vintage and presently in its revival phase. This is a rebound phase and hence entity can be considered as a strong one

- Point O3 and O7 indicates an entity in its maturity phase with strong and stable cash flows

- Point O4 indicates an entity in its declining phase with higher probability of dying out as there is no proven track record of revival

- Point O8 indicates an entity in its declining phase but has got history of bounce back as depicted by first cycle

I call this as an **"Inflection Point Analysis"** *which help us to identify the position of business on the IP curve at the time of review/enhancement/new acquisition of an asset.*

Movement of the entity from one point of the curve to other is influenced by either one or all of the following broad factors. These factors may alter the business growth path in the future and decide the curve for business:

1. Changes in government policies regarding the industry – can be a booster or dampener or can give space for substitutes to come

2. The overall economic condition of a nation influencing the demand of product being manufactured, changing working capital cycles of a business

3. The overall business environment is depressed leading to supply-side constraints

4. Transformation in Consumption pattern due to demographic changes

5. Thought process and future plans of the promoter – which may be either modification in business in sync with changing times or expansion of capacity or maybe diverging in an unrelated activity

Though all the five factors mentioned above are important, Factor 5 requires specific attention to get an understanding of business path in future. Top 4 factors are external and influence the overall industry and the business. *On the other hand, Factor 5 is the response of promoter to first four factors.* **The response can be a non-reactive, reactive or proactive.**

Now the questions that arise here are:

1. How can we ascertain the stage of an entity? Where can we place the entity on **IP curve?** (See point A below)

2. How to judge the entity's future movement? How we know that entity will move from O2 to O3 and not directly from O2 to O5 (See point B below)

A. Stage of an entity on the IP curve is a function of:

-   **Vintage of business** – Entity at O5 will not be the same as the entity at O1. The entity at O1 is a start-up with not even financials for full-year or still waiting for breakeven to happen. On the other hand, the entity at O5 point will have n years of vintage which may commensurate with one industry cycle

-   **The number of cycles entity has passed through** – Entity at O2 is still at the initial stage of its cycle and passed through a breakeven phase in recent past. On the other hand, the entity at O6 stage has already seen one growth phase and one down phase with greater than n years of experience and may have passed through one industry cycle. Some entities can have a good vintage of say 7-8 years; however, they may not have gone through one full cycle of downfall and bounce back. *For this, we should have the right awareness about the previous cycles through which industry has passed through and have to superimpose an entity's life cycle on the particular industry cycles*

B. Future movement of an entity is a function of:

-   **Visibility of future Cash Flows** – This is a factor of entity's competitive position in the market, entity's linkage with suppliers and creditors and phase through which industry is passing and will pass through, in short to medium term

-   **Strength of balance sheet and management** – There has to be a strong support visible in balance sheet in the form of sufficient liquidity and low leverage which can enable the entity to brave the rough patch either through internal accruals or by raising funds. Additionally, promoters or group support and their reputation in the market plays a vital role in letting entity pass through these tough times

- **Future plans of the management** – Promoter's plan of expansion and diversification should be rightly timed and should also be duly supported by existing balance sheet fundamentals.

Consider two entities P and Q from same industry and both at the O2 stage:

(Value in Crores)

Parameters/ Entity	P			Q		
	201x	201y	201z	201x	201y	201z
Sales	100	115	127	100	150	200
EBIDTA	15%	15%	15%	5%	3%	6%
Debt	25	27	30	35	50	65
TNW	30	35	42	20	26	33
Debt/TNW (Ratio)	0.8	0.8	0.7	1.8	1.9	2
Current Ratio	1.7	1.8	1.9	1.3	1.2	1.2

Observation: Trajectory of growth for Q is quite fast however seems to be push sales by Q looking to quite thin margins vis a vis margins of P. Overall, entity P is quite strong and well placed in terms of liquidity and leverage and can survive short phase of disruption in the industry on its own and can survive longer phase also by raising funds owing to quite low leverage in the balance sheet. On the other hand, entity Q may face difficulty under these conditions. Hence, entity P in all probability will go from O2 to O3 or will remain at O2 position till there is an improvement in overall industry sentiment. However, there is a high probability for entity Q to go from point O2 to O5 directly during this down phase of the industry. Diagrammatically, the trajectory of P and Q can be represented by dotted lines on the Inflection Curve:

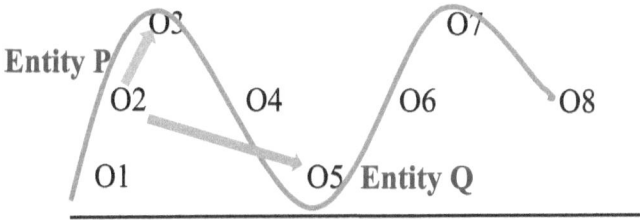

Awareness of the entity's position on Inflection curve, enable us to **"Time our decision Right"** *with respect to approval or denial of a proposition received.* Once, we are aware about the position of the business on the curve, we shall be able to position it in nine cube **"Business-Transaction Matrix."** This shall further enable us to decide the transactions suited to business so as to move it towards a stronger scenario and also able to decide the structure of mitigant.

I am providing here two cases to illustrate the point regarding future plans of the promoters as well as the responsiveness of the promoters to changing conditions:

CASE: A bank took over the client who was into export of specific food item to Europe for the last 10 years. Conduct of the existing bank was satisfactory at the time of takeover and the client was banking with them from last 4 year. At the time of the initial discussion, it came out that client's revenue from the food export in the last one year was stagnant. However, the total turnover of the firm was on an increasing trend due to two new business lines – Trading of imported household articles and distributorship of wooden wall tiles. Credit facilities were sanctioned for export of food items only. The client offered good collateral providing adequate coverage for the credit exposure.

Account operated satisfactorily for first one year and then onwards it started showing signs of liquidity constraints. During the stock audit done in mid-year it came to light that there was a high level of non-moving stock of wooden tiles and the long-pending receivables from the real estate projects. High receivables and high stocking led to liquidity problems to the firm affecting well-running activity of exporting food items, which was the main turnover churner for it.

It is an example of the thoughtlessness of promoter who was not able to ascertain the impact on the business segment it was diversifying and lacked preparedness to handle the adverse effect of new activity on the existing business. As a banker our learnings are:

Learning No 1 – Bank entered the relationship at the time when the client was entering into fairly new businesses where it has no prior experience

Learning No 2 – One of the businesses for the supply of wooden flooring was linked to real estate sector and the sector was not faring well due to oversupply and low demand

Learning No 3 – Do not get lured by available collaterals. Collaterals are only a mitigant and can never be a comfort for taking credit exposure.

CASE: Bank A had a client B who was into packaging and printing business for two decades. B was banking with bank A from last 5 years and banking conduct was satisfactory.

Client's 70% of business was coming from manufacturing plastic pouches for pan masala companies. In 2011, the Supreme Court ordered a ban on the sale of pan masala in plastic pouches. This came as a sudden shock to B as Supreme Court order provided very less breather time.

What differentiated B from many other players in the industry was their proactive approach. B was one of the first to have a discussion with its customers to look for alternate paper packaging solutions. In the meantime, it also started discussion with customers from different industries to mitigate its concentration risk. These were the industries where polythene packaging was permitted and B could use existing setup to supply products.

At the same time, B went ahead and put up additional assemblies for paper-based packaging for its pan masala clients. For this B got adequate support from the bank A though there were instances of overdue in the account due to vacuum of orders from major business segment. Within 6 months, B recovered from the partial setback and was on track.

The above was an example of a client with a proactive approach and a good support system to sustain surprises in the business.

In addition to what we have seen in the chapter till now, I would like to provide perspective on what more need to be done in brown field/green filed/start up project funding. For these scenarios my approach is based on the **"Tunnel Concept."** Let us see an example to understand the concept:

CASE: Bank A has received a proposition to fund a start-up. This is a new business and so there are no financials available to analyze. Promoters are also foraying in this business for the first time and they have also to test the waters.

Promoters are High Net worth Individuals and are offering good collateral to adequately cover the exposure requested. Other positive is, regular income of promoters from the other running businesses. Income from other businesses is enough to take care of periodic repayment obligations of proposed start-up till the time of break even. However, the point of concern is slow down in existing business in the last 2 years and reduction in the valuation of the existing company.

Products under proposed business are quite new for the market and hence awareness among people is not high. On the positive side, government policies are quite supportive and there is all-round support from the government in terms of lower taxes and creation of infrastructure for the product. Now, the question is – Should we or should we not go-ahead for funding this new venture.

As I said, I will follow the tunnel concept (Fig below). In respect of synonymy, '**Tunnel**' implies period starting from the date of disbursement of debt and ending to the point where entity achieves break-even and is capable to service debt. Since, this business is based on a new concept, *Tunnel's length is a function of* **adaptability of product in the market, company's distribution capability** *and* **continuance of government's support for the industry**.

X is a point of commencement of business; Y is a point on a day on which project achieve breakeven; Z is a new date of break even in case of delays.

To take care of smooth journey through this tunnel and to see the light on the other end, there need to be cash flow support for the business by the promoters. This support is required till the time business has enough cash flow to take care of debt obligation on its own. It is also important to factor in any exigencies like delay in commencement of production or lower than the expected income of promoters from other businesses whose cash flows were expected to support new business till the end of a tunnel. *This exceptional situation requires a strong net worth of promoters as a backup which I call "Pit Support."*

Additionally, once we are convinced on the viability of the project and have measured the length of the tunnel properly, we can adopt the ballooning method of repayment to take care of initial hiccups in the project.

It is important to analyze the proposition of capacity expansion (both brownfield or green field) from both **"In Tunnel"** as well as **"After Tunnel"** perspective i.e. once project passed through the tunnel. *Analysis requires correct projections of cash flow generation from the proposed project, cash flow support from the existing activity and capability of promoters to support the project in case of time overrun.*

In some of the scenarios, it is observed that customer put new projects only for availing the advantage of taxation and subsidies provided for a specific sector. Hence, it is pertinent to understand the existing capacity utilization and the envisaged demand for the future. Is the capital expenditure going to add any additional capacity or is it being put up to improve the overall efficiency? It is also important to check the residual period of government advantages available to the entity, which should be well above our term debt repayment period. Also need to carry sensitivity analysis on repayment coverage calculations from cash flow generation without considering government benefits like interest subsidy, income tax/excise exemptions, electricity subsidy etc.

There was a period when people did a good amount of investments in some areas of the country like Baddi especially in the pharma segment. Post announcement of benefits in 2003, the region saw opening up of a good number of small and medium pharma units catering to both domestic and export markets. Big multinational clients diverted their orders to these entities due to cheaper sourcing as a result of excise and income tax exemptions along with capital subsidy. However, post expiry of excise and income tax exemption some of the individuals who put up units with sole objective of taking these benefits, find it unviable to continue their operations.

Similarly, in the textile segment, some of the players went ahead for capital expansion merely to stake advantage of TUF scheme. We observed cases where client came with the proposal to put up capacities much larger than the existing capacity with no clear vision and strategy on the distribution of excess production in the market.

Sometimes, customers put a food processing unit under subsidy schemes of Ministry of Food Processing Industries (MOFPI). However, this is done without preparedness to bring additional funds in case of delayed subsidy receipts. This leads to extension in project commencement or in a worse situation may stall the project halfway.

We have also observed, clients, going ahead with capacity expansion dedicated for one principal which normally happens in some segments like Auto, FMCG, Food processing etc. I will take you through one more real-life example to explain the inherent risk in this structure.

CASE: Bank ABC had a client who was into manufacturing of FMCG products for the big multinational brand. The client was producing and selling products under own brand also and was a listed entity. Promoters were doing well in the market and have good relationship with the multinational principal. The client was approached by the same multinational principal for putting up a dedicated facility to do contract manufacturing of a new product to be introduced in the Indian market. The client put up a facility which was quite bigger than the existing one, and the capital outlay was also substantial compared to existing net worth.

There was assured offtake of product from the principal for initial 2 years from the date of commencement of production. It was not enough to cover up the debt repayment on standalone basis though the visibility of debt payment was there considering cash flows from existing business also. Everything went well for the next 3 years till the principal decided to discontinue the product in the Indian market. This led to the stoppage of production from the plant and hence fall in turnover of the company on an overall basis. Eventually, account turned delinquent due to non-repayment of debt.

Contrary to the above, I have seen clients who themselves are conscious about risk due to dependency on a single principal. Though they may have started initially with dependency on a single customer, they add on other principals in their portfolio with time to have a diversified customer base. Even in the cases where they have a dependency on a single customer, they try to have multiple product line supplies to reduce the concentration risk.

There can be a scenario when we receive proposition with a good track record but going forward promoters may have future plans which may or may not be conducive to overall business. *Scenarios discussed in the chapter shows that what makes a difference is the approach of promoters towards business going forward and identification of the inflection point by us at the time of underwriting.*

Chapter 4

Completing 360° View

What all is required to gain complete understanding of the customer and about the exposure we are going to have? We have already discussed the factors influencing business, the role of transactions and mitigants to strengthen the proposal and about the timing of entering into a relationship.

One of an important activity which completes our **360°** vision is **due diligence** about the client and its business.

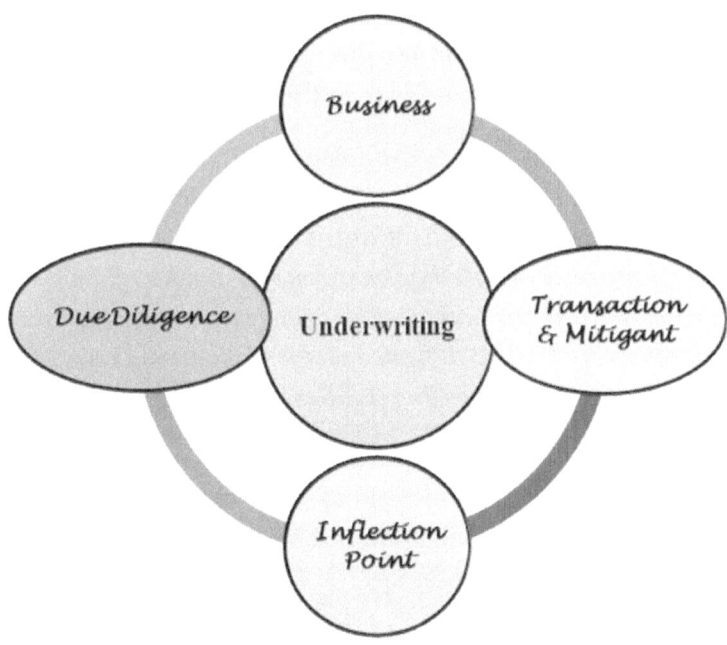

Due diligence on client comprises of three activities required to be done at every phase of business relationship:

1. Market reference – *MORE* (**Market Opinion Regarding Entrepreneur**)

2. KYC

3. Dedupe Checks

It is convenient to get information on clients who are rated by the credit rating agencies. For clients in smaller business segments, especially in SME, who are unrated, extraction of information happens through comprehensive KYCs, extended dedupes and informal channels like a Market reference.

Comprehensive KYC entails going beyond normal KYC required for starting the liability relationship. And extended dedupes means dedupes of not only the entity whom we are funding but also dedupes for group entities, their promoters, their guarantors and whosoever has a strategic say in the business.

KYC and dedupes provide complete understanding about the client and their standing in the market. They are the first wall of defence and are integral and indispensable for good underwriting. *Analysis and recommendations on a proposal can vary from person to person but dedupes and other due diligence are the actualities about the account and there is no room for committing error. They are Go-No-Go for on-boarding the client.*

Doing KYC and dedupes on the client is an integral part of credit underwriting. However, sometimes we overlook and miss to touch base some of the vital points. I have observed some of the common miss outs like:

> **We left out** – We missed dedupes of some guarantors, group entities etc

> **We keep open** – For old events, though we report them as negative dedupes, we do not add our clarification or remarks and keep them open

> **We assume** – In some instances, though we take cognizance of negative dedupes, we do not report the same assuming amount to be small and immaterial

Since, these are the facts to be reported, we do not have liberty to be selective. All of them need to be reported and supported with facts, and proper justification need to be provided for going ahead with the credit. In fact, I have observed that these factors make large pie of reasons reported for staff accountability.

Every institution has its policy and processes which defines the sources to be used for doing due diligence. They also define the framework within which dedupes need to be carried. In case, it is not there, then it is better to make the framework and define standards at the earliest to evade ambiguity. For a business and credit analyst it is sacrosanct to follow policy guidelines. However, this is what is minimum required to be done as per policy. We should explore beyond it if the situation warrants.

I did discussion with analysts to ascertain reasons for 3 miss outs mentioned above, and the most common statement made by them was *"client was reluctant to provide information."*

Now the questions we need to ask ourselves here are –

1. Are we asking too much of information from client?

2. Can we not extract part information from available online portals or government sites?

3. What can be termed as critical and what as non-critical information?

4. Should we go ahead with credit in case the client refuses to provide critical information?

5. How much information can be termed as Optimum Information?

Let us see the following flow chart:

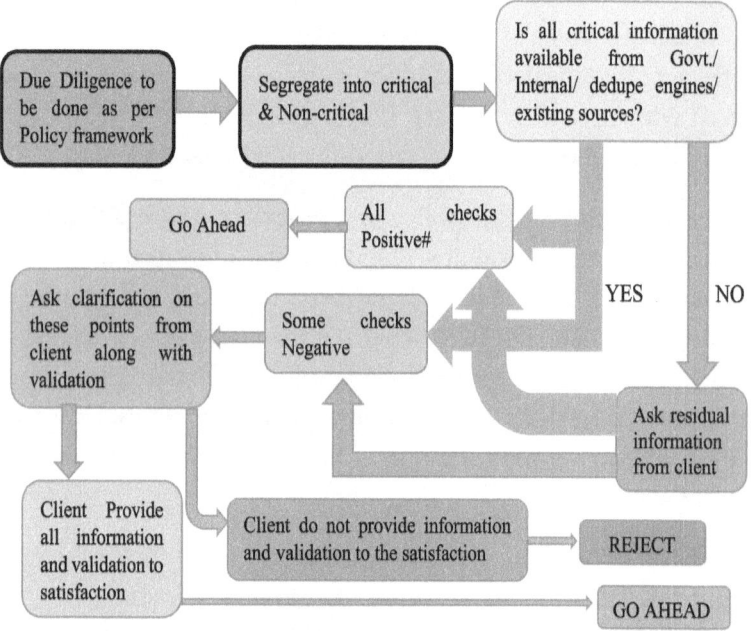

Positive implies – No negative news about client

Flow chart guarantees that we do not miss out on the minimum due diligence required to take credit decision. It also ensures minimum mining of information from the client thus ensuring better turnaround time and less hassle for client.

The client may not share information, not with an intent to hide something but sometimes, clients may be irate due to substantial information asked which is not contextual. Make your checklist to decide criticality of information required. Segregate information into Critical and Non-Critical using your prudence which ensures going through optimal information only for the decision. *As a general rule, information which is "Must have" is Critical and "Good to have" information is Non-critical.*

We can extract information about the client from available public sources, market information and available dedupe reports. Post that, whatever unanswered and is **"critically required"** need to be asked from client. *If the client avoids providing critical information, then that is the "point of not going ahead."*

CASE: Bank A sanctioned working capital exposure to a client P who use to provide technical consultancies and do EPC work for big government & MNC clients. The client was disbursed working capital limits in the form of cash credit and performance bank guarantees. The client had a good track record for execution of contracts. Financials were also robust with low leverage and year to year growth of turnover in the last 3-4 year. Promoters were well-qualified as required for the trade of business. Everything was positive, including the industry in which the company was operating and hence exposure was sanctioned as per the requirement.

Account ran well for 4 months till the bank received information regarding one of the operational creditors going into NCLT against the company for non-payment of dues. During the course of review of the account, it came to the notice that the bank had taken cognizance of this overdue creditor at the time of sanction itself. However, looking to the overall comfortable net worth of company these outstanding creditors were considered a normal event and sanction provided.

Post event analysis reveal that company has executed one overseas contract wherein there was back to back arrangement with the supplier for payment. However, customer did not enter into written agreement with the supplier as this was a regular supplier to the company and was associated with it from last 3 years. Since, there was substantial delay in completion of contract due to delays from the principal it caused pain for suppliers also as the contract was big and supplier payment was also substantial. Hence, supplier filed case in NCLT against P and this was done during the process of sanction. Account turned NPA due to overdue as a result of hold on the operations and delayed receipts from the principal.

Let's summarize the case for learnings which can be drawn from it –

Learning 1 – Further due diligence was required to be done on overdue creditor as size was not small. Could have talked to the creditor to understand the issue

Learning 2 – Due diligence on contract where there were delays could have been done at the pre sanction stage itself. Client was doing 2-3 contracts at any point of time and these were all big projects with varying duration of 12-18 months. Could have checked the progress and payments from this project especially when supplier payments from the same contract was long due

Learning 3 – Missed on pre checks on operational creditors from NCLT perspective

Above was the situation where bank missed the critical dedupe by assuming that everything will be right as client has good track and satisfactory financials. However, this small slip led to a larger problem which was not even thought of.

I am giving another example here to exhibit the situation where analyst identified the issue and asked for the relevant information. However, client declined to provide the same. This corroborate the statement made earlier in the chapter – If client avoid providing critical information then that is the **"Point of not going ahead."**

CASE: Bank B had a client Q who manufacture flexible packaging and was dealing with bank from last 2 years with satisfactory operations and conduct. At the time of third renewal client put up a request for enhancement which was not in sync with the growth in last 2 years. There was no satisfactory reason from client for requirement of additional limits except threat to exit relationship in absence of incremental exposure. During 2-3 rounds of interaction with the client and information from the market, banker came to know that client is setting up a new business with his friends and cousin for manufacturing Food grade films.

Further deliberations revealed that there were four partners with an equal stake of 25% each for a project. The project was approximately 4 times the capacity of an existing business of a client and initial capital outlay was also large. To understand more, the banker asked for details of the project, its financial outlay, financial closures and overall contribution. Banker also asked for details of businesses of other partners however client turned down the request. *These details were necessarily required to understand promoter contribution in the new project, which may lead to the diversion of funds from existing business.*

Banker also tried to understand about client's engagement required in other business which may affect existing business. It was also important to understand the capability of other promoters to bring fund in case there is time and cost overrun in the project or in case financial closure does not happen.

Since the banker could not get the details to carry due diligence, they rejected enhancement. The client exited a relationship and was provided enhanced limits from the competition. In the next 6-7 months of enhancement, account started showing sign of stress like hard-core utilization, a slowdown in business, overdue in account and account turned NPA within one renewal cycle. Reason, diversion of fund by promoters and most of their energy being utilized for pushing off new project.

Lesson: *Decision based on known facts is taking a "risk." Decision without considering information critical to take a decision is like entering into an unknown terrain and is nothing short of making a bet.*

Doing KYC and dedupes for the account ensure in-depth due diligence by using available online sources and bureau records. *However, one informal channel which provides information on a real-time basis much before it is available through formal dedupe sources is* **"Market Reference."** I have named this process as **"MORE"** which stands for *Market Opinion Regarding Entrepreneur.* Market reference can be obtained from suppliers, customers, peers, financiers and even the employees. Market reference is part of KYC but we can discuss it separately looking to its importance in the overall credit process.

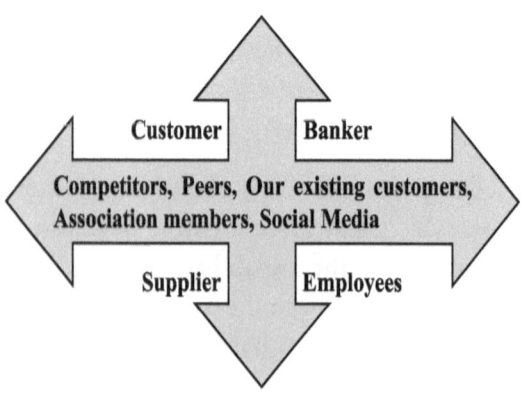

MORE (Both way Referencing – Vertical & Lateral)

As we say that the more, the merrier, a greater amount of referencing in both vertical and lateral fashion will always be better. Few points which I would like to emphasis in respect of Market reference are:

- ✐ **Multidimensional** – As the above diagram shows, take reference checks from both categories of sources. One, who are directly associated (Supplier etc.) in the supply chain and others who are indirectly associated (Competitors, etc.) as a group

- ✐ **Extensive** – Reference checks should be done as extensively as possible. It has to be done from multiple suppliers, multiple customers and other multiple sources. This will help nullify the bias of referencing sources towards the client

- ✐ **Never-ending** – Market reference is not a one-time activity. It requires continuous probing at regular intervals so as to capture early warning signals much ahead of evident stress in the account

- ✐ **Sources** – Important is the source from which we obtain the references. It has to be Authentic, unbiased one

- ✐ **Guarded** – Market reference for the client need to be restricted for official consumption and not to be revealed to anybody else

CASE: Bank ABC had a client PQR with a satisfactory relationship of 3 years. Satisfactory in terms of growing top line and no overdue, however, account used to have hard-core utilization of limits. Promoters were into the trading business from last 16 years. In between, after 2 years of satisfactory operations, the account was provided with an enhancement by the bank basis year on year increase in the top line. Financials were also in line with other traders in the same industry segment. There were no adverse remarks in dedupe reports for the entity as well as the promoters.

One good day there came abrupt halt of credits in the bank accounts and in the next 90 days account turned NPA. On inquiry, the client informed that there was IT raid which has disrupted the business. This led to chaos in the market, leading the creditors to call their money back from the client. Inspection of warehouse of client showed very less stock available which, according to the client, was taken away by the creditors.

However, reference from peers revealed that promoter availed high interest linked unsecured loans from the market. Discussion with the client revealed that they raised loans from unsecured lenders (from informal segment) for investment in the real estate. These loans were raised much before they started a relationship with bank ABC. Later on, due to slow down in the market, it became difficult to sell the property. Client resort to incremental lending from other unsecured lenders at a higher rate to pay off existing high rate unsecured loans on their maturity. Vicious circle led to a high burden of debt serviceability on the client.

The question here is—If the client had incremental turnover year on year, then why he was not in a position to service and pay the market debt?

Deep dive into the account by the bank officials made it clear that promoter was dealing with 3-4 customers only and sale-purchase was happening with the same set of clients. Out of these set of customers, one of the customers XYZ was an existing client of bank ABC. In fact, client PQR was onboarded by a bank basis reference provided by XYZ.

Learning: *Though nothing was missed in terms of dedupe, what was lacked was market intelligence at the time of boarding the client. Another aspect where bank could have done better was market references on regular interval, which could have provided early signals of stress.* **Though market reference checks are generally obtained at the time of boarding, "regular reference checks from the market is important."** *Thirdly, the bank obtained reference check from an existing clients who were either supplier or customer of the client. It was important for the bank to have reference checks from peers, competitors and clients in another industry segment also.*

Chapter 5

Monitoring Essentials

During one of my interactions with young credit managers, one enthusiastic gentleman asked – "What is the role and responsibilities of Credit Manager." I paused for a second and then in reciprocation, I asked them two questions.

Question No 1: Do our role as a credit manager is limited up to sanction stage?

Question No 2: Do we or do we not, agree with the above statement?

There was pin-drop silence for a moment. I was confident that there is an answer in the room and that will come from my young team members only. After a while, people started raising hands—one, then two, then three, and so on and in a couple of minutes, most of the young faces were smiling and were eager to answer. I know that answer will be – *"none of us agrees with this view"*. And yes, I was right in my prediction. As a good Credit Manager, it is important to have good monitoring skills along with good underwriting skill sets.

Right underwriting ensures good credit to enter into the system. However, we cannot be sure about the behaviour of account or portfolio in future as the scenario under which we have underwritten the credit may not be the same in the future. *Hence, it requires ongoing monitoring of an underwritten portfolio.*

There are several MISs in the organisation which provide indication of cases going into stress however the information comes with lag. We require to have extended approach wherein we can as a precursor identify the triggers for stress well in advance so that we can act before it starts taking toll on the liquidity of a company.

Overall, it needs to be a three-pronged strategy as demonstrated in the diagram. I call it **"Skeleton of Monitoring."** There are three sources of triggers namely – MIS of an organisation (name it X), Sources other than formal MIS (name it Y) and Event-based triggers (name it Z). We shall be gaining understanding about Skeleton of Monitoring as we progress in our discussion in the chapter.

The Skeleton of Monitoring

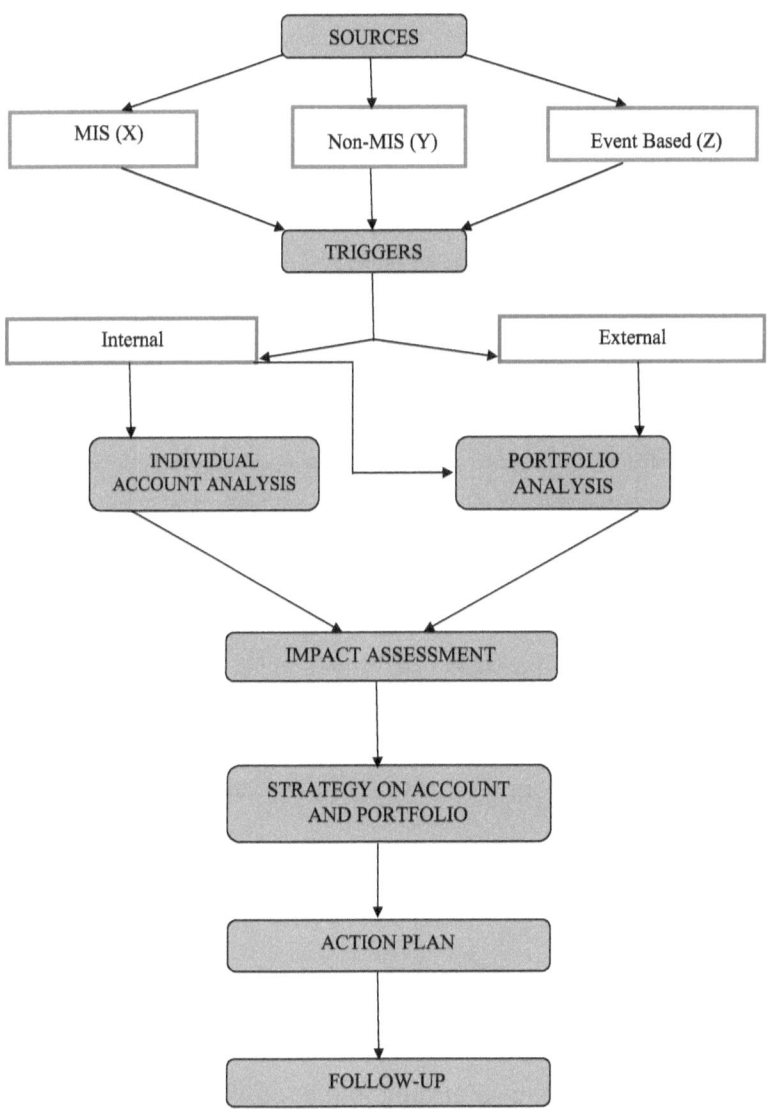

We need to keep tab *simultaneously and consistently* on all the three sources which can provide triggers of stress in the account. *It requires us to see all of them together so that we do not miss on the critical indicators.*

Different organisations have MISs related to the monitoring of the portfolio. These may have different names but have the same Core – they all revolve around the conduct of account like overdue, non-servicing of interest, a bounce of instalments, etc. Additionally, there are Early Warning Signals (EWS) MISs which throws light on behavioural aspects of account like utilization pattern, cheque returning, frequency of TODs, delayed stock statement submission etc.

EWS – MIS (X1) is a precursor to Other – MIS (X2) on delinquencies (See Fig A).

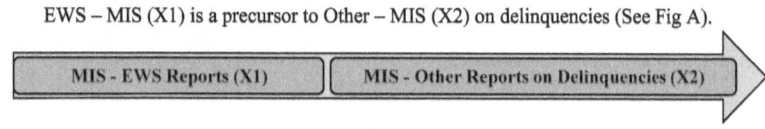

Fig A

EWS-MIS (X1) provides warning signals of stress through available account conduct information. Other-MIS (X2) like overdue reports, delayed servicing of interest etc are result of liquidity constraint in the entity and *is the last stage to act for us.*

Consider a scenario where account starts showing:

- Delayed submission of stock statement
- Delayed Stock/Receivables Audit
- Frequent TODs in the account
- High Cheque returning in the account
- LC devolvement/BG invocation

- Recurring Hard Core Utilization of limits

- High cash withdrawals in the account

- Lower than expected credits in the account

- Account though may be good with us but bad with other banks/FIs. It may be doing good with us for the time being but can be SMA/NPA with others

Above are Early Warning signals which may or may not be accompanied with overdue/interest delay/instalment delays (All are Other-MIS (X2)). *As a Credit Manager, we need to have action at least at this stage as beyond this point, we shall have very squeezed action-time to take corrective measures.*

Other scenarios are where account display following behaviour:

- Recurring overdues in the account

- Credits in the account less than the debits

- Delayed instalment payments

Above are resultants of strained liquidity in the account and are reported through Other-MIS (X2). These can appear subsequent to evident Early Warning Signs in the account or can appear simultaneously or can be a result of some event (will discuss ahead) wherein there is no Early Warning Sign in the account. Important actionable on our part is to prevent account flowing in higher DPD (days past due) bucket through recoveries and finally finding a resolution.

Now let us modify Fig A which we shall call as Fig B.

| Non-MIS (Y) | MIS - EWS Reports (X1) | MIS - Other Reports on Delinquency (X2) |

Fig B

We have added another source of triggers, which we call as Non-MIS (Y) as this is a source of information which is normally not captured in the available EWS or other delinquency MISs in the organisation. This is where our market intelligence, our quest for finding indicators of stress by going beyond available MIS, our understanding of portfolio and customers comes into play. Non-MIS sources are the precursor to reporting's under MISs available in the organisation which provide the status of overdues and early-warning signals. *So, they are one step before even EWS is get captured in MIS*

Before going further into discussion, let us take the real-life example to substantiate the previous statement.

CASE: Bank A had a customer B who was into the business of Sports equipment. B was a wholesaler and retailer of some of the marquee brands in the sports industry. The client was there with the bank in multiple banking for 6 years with satisfactory conduct in all the banks.

In between client strategically decided to enter into the business of Sports Health Supplements. Looking to the past business vintage, positive industry scenario, satisfactory conduct in the account, the bank provided B additional funding for this line of business. Overall, client was doing good business, and the account performance was also satisfactory with regular credits in the bank.

At the time of next renewal (client requested for enhancement also) bank found some anomaly related to credits in the account. Banker made a market inquiry from the suppliers and peers as well as from some of the existing customers of the bank who were operating from the same market place. Banker got the information that B is raising funds from the market and is delaying payment to some of the suppliers. Banker also got information from the market that B has entered into business partnership overseas for production of health supplements however B denied the same. Basis above feedback bank carried receivable and stock audits which also revealed some anomalies for which client could not provide satisfactory answers.

Bank declined enhancement to the client and gave indications of exit *though there was no evident sign of stress from account conduct*. Client raised credit from other FI at enhanced levels and exited from bank A. After a year's time of exiting relationship, B defaulted on credit from another bank.

Above example demonstrates that though all MISs {both EWS (X1) as well as delinquency MIS (X2)} were giving the right picture of the account at that point of time, there were Non-MIS (Y) sources which provided triggers of stress in an entity.

This is a scenario where account display following behaviour:

- ✍ Adverse reference/Adverse news in the market about the promoters/entity. This may be related to financials or non-financials reasons. Non-financial reasons can be related to a dispute between the promoters or about the health of main promoters and so on

- ✍ Raising unsecured loans from the market and financial institutions

- ✍ Adverse comments in Audit reports about the contingent liabilities

- ✍ Adverse comments in Stock/Receivable Audits

- ✍ Increase in working capital cycles

- ✍ Increase in inquiries for loans in Dedupes

- ✍ Change in scope of projects put up for expansion

- ✍ Delay in submission of required information for renewal or review of the account

- ✍ Adverse observations in the account statement – Circular transactions, Round entries, related party transactions

- ✍ Non-payment of statutory dues/delay in GST payments

- ✍ Change in demand for the products dealt by an entity

Identification of above scenarios require a constant subjective analysis of the accounts and the portfolio. It requires quick anticipation of adverse situations and fast turnaround time to prevent account displaying EWS and overdue behaviour. It is pertinent to have a discussion with the client to reach to the core of the problems before reaching to any conclusion. Sometimes, the above actions may not be the result of constrained liquidity but may be due to ignorance of client or genuine business growth requirements.

Following are some of the situations which require exclusive mention as they are easy to capture our attention and are the first point of actionable:

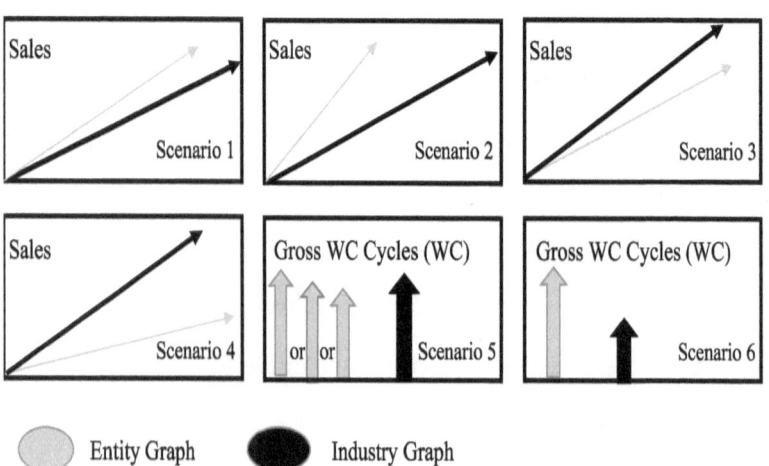

Scenario 1 in combination with Scenario 6	Require further investigation *(Sales is better than industry average)* *(WC is quite high vis a vis industry average – Maybe a push sales)*
Scenario 2 in combination with Scenario 5	Require further investigation *Very sharp growth rate vis a vis industry; however, WC is in line with industry average which may be due to:* *Very efficient processor or,* *There can be a situation of circular transactions or over trade*
Scenario 2 in combination with Scenario 6	Require further investigation *(Sales is better than industry average)* *(WC is quite high vis a vis industry average – Maybe a push sale)*
Scenario 3 in combination with Scenario 5	No action required *(Sales is more or so in line with industry average)* *(WC is also in line with industry average)*
Scenario 3 in combination with Scenario 6	Require further investigation and immediate action *(Sales is more or so in line with industry average)* *(WC is quite high vis a vis industry average)*
Scenario 4 in combination with Scenario 5	Critical situation and require immediate remedial measures *(Sales has seen a sharp fall as compared to industry average)* *(WC is still in tandem with industry average)*
Scenario 4 in combination with Scenario 6	Critical situation and require immediate remedial measures *(Sales has seen sharp fall as compared to industry average)* *(WC is quite high vis a vis industry average)*

Now let us now modify figure B which we shall call as Fig C

Fig C

We have now added Event-Based Source of triggers. Like Non-MIS sources, Event-Based is also a precursor to both EWS and Other reports on delinquency. Event-based triggers are abrupt events and provide us with very less time to react. These can be one or some of the following triggers:

- Government Policy announcement about the sector

- Raw Material prices fluctuations

- Forex fluctuation, if the entity is import or export dependent

- Labour unrest or any major accident at the unit

- The demise of main promoters

- Force majeure

During 2014-15 we all have seen a sharp decline in the prices of oils to the extent of 50% in the international market. This was an event which affected clients in the oil industry and the clients who were in the business of oil derivatives. It was a sharp decline in the prices of oil and affected portfolio of our clients who were into the business of polymers. These were the players who were majorly into the import and the trading of the polymers. As the prices declined sharply, clients were forced to sell their high-priced inventory at a much lower price leading to losses on those transactions.

All the triggers (X1, X2, Y and Z) we discussed can be a result of factors which are either internal or external to an entity. For example, the dispute between the promoters is a factor internal to an entity and is going to affect the performance of a particular entity only. On the other hand, change in the prices of oil is a factor external to an entity and will affect all the entities engaged in the trade of oil and oil derivatives.

It is important to observe the strings emanating from the identified factor. If the trigger is a result of external factors, then it warrants for Portfolio review as ramification can be widespread across the particular industry, geography, trade etc. It is also important to see whether the identified factor will affect the whole supply chain in lateral fashion or vertical fashion or can affect whole structure within a particular industry domain. *Accordingly, our scope of review is decided.* Let us see some of the scenarios related to external factors (there can be several one)

Scenario A: Increase in price of cotton

Consequences:

1. It may affect both traders of cotton and traders of cotton yarns

2. It may affect manufacturers of garments

3. It may affect both domestic entities as well as exporters

Review Span: Will require a portfolio review of all the accounts in the Textile Portfolio

Scenario B: Increase in price of Oil

Consequences:

1. It may affect traders and manufacturers of polymers

2. It may affect manufacturers of plastic products

3. It may affect manufacturers of paints

4. It may affect manufacturers of plastic packaging material

Review Span: Will require portfolio review of accounts in polymer, paint, packaging, other sectors present in supply chain of oil and oil derivatives

Scenario C: Downgrade of the rating of particular Corporate by an external rating agency

Consequences:

1. It may affect our clients who are vendors/suppliers to that corporate

2. It may affect our clients who are dealers/customers of that corporate

Review Span: Will require only some client-specific reviews

Scenario D: Change in government policies by the state government with respect to a particular industrial area

Consequences:

1. It may affect the accounts in the portfolio from a particular industrial area

2. It may affect all other accounts who are indirectly linked to the clients in that geography

Review Span:

1. Review of all the accounts in a particular geography

2. Review of past actionable of the state government to establish a pattern

All the above scenarios are examples of External Triggers basis which we take account specific actions. However, on the other hand, there can also be the factors which seemingly are internal to an entity however deeper insight may lead to the conclusion that factor may have a widespread effect on particular industry, trade or geography.

Let us see some of those scenarios also:

Scenario E: Receipt of IT inquiries in some accounts post demonetization

Consequences:

1. It may lead to action by IT authorities against the management of these entities

2. It may affect accounts from a particular industry or trade

Review Span:

1. Review of past notices to establish trend across industry or trade

2. Portfolio review of all industries and trades where trend get established

3. Review of all the accounts to pick management specific trends

Scenario F: A drop in the valuation of properties in some cases

Consequences:

1. It may lead to a reduction of security in particular accounts

2. It may lead to reduced security coverage in accounts from a particular geography

3. It may lead to a reduction in valuations done by particular valuators

Review Span:

1. Review of all these valuations to establish trend across different geographies

2. Review of all these valuations to seek out trend for particular valuator

Scenario G: Labour unrest in a particular unit

Consequences:

1. It may lead to disruption in the production of a particular unit

2. It may be widespread labour unrest in a particular geography

3. It may be a trend building up in a particular industry

Review Span:

1. Review of a particular unit to understand the expanse of an issue. Whether it is management-specific or geography related union issues

2. Review of some entities from the same industry located in a different geography. This is to establish an industry-specific trend

Scenario H: Increase in Working Capital Cycles of an entity

Consequences:

1. It may be specific to an entity

2. It may be a trend across a particular industry

Review Span:

1. Review of a particular unit

2. Review of some other entities from the same industry to establish an industry-specific trend

Scenario I: Decrease in the top line of an entity

Consequences:

1. It may be specific to an entity

2. It may be a trend across particular industry

Review Span:

1. Review of particular unit

2. Review of some other entities from same industry to establish industry specific trend

All the above scenarios discussed have factors which have widespread consequences and hence warranted for Portfolio Review. In general, all the triggers from External Factors will require Portfolio Review and are quite observable. They may be event based or non-event based. On the other hand, all triggers from internal factors may have genesis within the entity/ management and is restricted to particular account only. However, sometimes micro analysis of a trigger reveals that though issue is seemingly internal to an entity but the genesis lies somewhere in external domain. Hence this scenario warrants for Portfolio Review as we have seen in scenarios E to I.

Scenarios like demise of promoter, delayed submission of stock statements, adverse comments in stock audit etc are triggers confined to internal factors and hence require individual account analysis

As I mentioned earlier, it is very important for us to gauge through the complete chain connected to the account identified for review. It shall be an approach which leads us from Microanalysis to identify the evolving Macro trend. So, it is like starting from the tip of the pyramid and then going down towards the base to cover a broader population (Fig D).

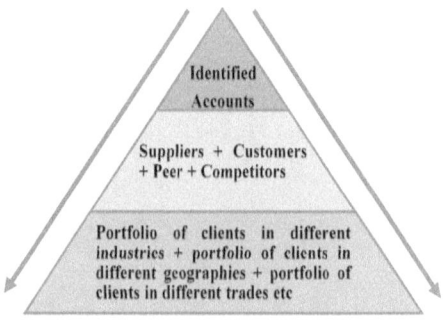

Fig D - Pyramid Approach

On the other hand, we have Inverted Pyramid approach (Fig E) where we shall analyse the Macro trends which can affect Portfolios in general and then will pin the accounts within the portfolio requiring critical account wise review and formation of strategy thereon.

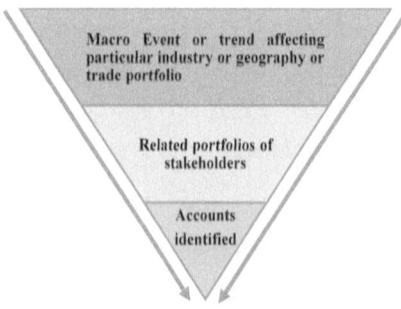

Fig E - Inverted Pyramid Approach

Once, we have identified the review levels and extent to which we need to cover, we need to analyse the Impact of event or non-event factors on the account and overall portfolio so as to ring-fence the expected losses. Once we have done Impact Assessment, we need to have account wise or portfolio (as the case may be) wise strategy to mark accounts/Portfolio as Close Monitoring for particular period, Reduction of our exposure, Enhanced collateralization, Rehabilitation, Restructuring etc.

Whenever we carry out Impact Assessment on the identified set of accounts, we have to bear in mind that not all entities will be affected in a similar fashion due to an identified cause. The extent to which entities will be affected will depend on their inherent strength and management quality. Accordingly, the probability of accounts moving in from better rating to lower ratings will vary. *And this will lead to our differential strategies on accounts facing similar situation unless we have decided to have common a Portfolio-based actionable.*

Any Strategy on Account will be successful only when we have right implementation and monitoring of timelines. We need to have optimum Action Plan with both Reduction/Action Milestones on the decided timelines. More important is then to monitor the progress and strong Follow-Up with the respective stakeholders through periodic MISs on it.

Chapter 6

Compliance, Controls and Audits

"Banks must stress good compliance culture, as the compliance in the system is far from satisfactory" – Mr. M.K. Jain, Deputy Governor, RBI, said at FIBAC 2019, Annual Global Banking Conference organised by IBA and FICCI, Mumbai (ET: Aug 20, 2019)

"It won't be an exaggeration to say that some of the big losses suffered by banks on account of frauds could have been avoided if good **compliance culture** was ingrained," he said (ET: Aug 20, 2019)

As per RBI, in FY19, Indian banking system detected total 3,766 (15% over FY18) incidents of frauds totalling to ₹71,500 crores (80% over FY18).

From June 2018 to July 2019, the Reserve Bank imposed monetary penalties on 76 occasions amounting to ₹122.9 crore on various commercial banks operating in India.

Investopedia describe Compliance department as bank's internal police force. Consider two situations:

City A	City B
1. Very strict compliance by Police for citizen's security	1. Very strict compliance by Police for citizen's security
2. Low awareness among residents	2. High awareness among residents

In above two situations, you can easily predict that incidences of crime will certainly be low in case of City B. Reason is simple;

- Since, residents are aware about possible crime situations, they are cautious and their rate of crime aversion shall be high

- Criminals shall always be hesitant and will think twice before performing crime as they are aware about the preparedness of citizens. Psychology plays its role here

Now, let's take an analogy to the above situation where we replace cities with banks and residents with bank's employees. The message is very clear – irrespective of how strong is our compliance department, factors which make difference is the:

- ✓ **Awareness** of employees about regulatory and organisational norms, rules, regulations, policies and processes

- ✓ **Adherence** to these norms, rules and regulations

And the above two are possible only when the organisation has a good **"Compliance Culture."**

What are the actionable required at our (employee) level so as to have desired compliance culture in an organisation? In my opinion, broadly, I will say that we all need to follow below practices religiously, which shall ensure the optimum level of compliance adherence:

- ✍ Keep your checklist ready for do's and don'ts in respect of processes and policies

- ✍ Analyse and act swiftly on observations raised by Auditors and internal Hindsight teams. As a leader, run a training session for team based on learnings from past Audits

- ✍ Look for OR event and report them quickly to the OR team (Those are starting point for frauds)

- ✍ Close monitoring of all the accounts from RFA standpoint

- ✍ Keep your eyes and ears open for suspicious activity either by the customer or any other stakeholder

Above is not an exhaustive list of actionable but it covers a substantial part of the universe.

Banks have an Internal Audits to keep a check on the errors which we make in the daily course of business. Scope of Audit involves taking out observation on the end-to-end process from sourcing to underwriting to disbursement and then monitoring of the portfolio. I have observed that sometimes we are too obsessed to close the observations raised by Audit. Contrary to this, we need to analyse and understand the reasons for the mistake and set the course for modification required in processes, policies and practices being carried up till now. Also need to make a checklist basis observation raised by the auditors and make it as a part of training so as to avoid mistakes in future.

In my duration as a leader, I have come across the situations where Stock Auditor raised some observations in respect of lesser drawing power (DP), but both relationship manager and an analyst missed it without any explanation being called from the client and no corrective action is taken. Stock Inspection is one of the most important monitoring tools and provides the right perspective about the operations in the company funded. Sometimes, it is observed that Stock Auditor has asked for some information from the client, but client either delay in providing information or do not provide information at all and Stock Auditor have to provide qualified reports. For an analyst, it is important to identify those cases with negative comments and the cases with qualified reports for review. The review provides a correct perspective about the account and also enable to provide a word of caution to the client that its conduct is closely monitored. This enables avoidance of diversion of funds and inculcates discipline for the future in the client. Let us see two cases to substantiate the above point:

CASE – Bank LMN had a client ABC who was into import as well as the local purchase of steel for further selling it into the local market. ABC use to purchase steel scrap from the large corporates and also use to import special grade steel. ABC always maintained a large quantity of stock as it used to procure steel through the auction process and also use to pick big volumes from imports so as to have pricing arbitrage. ABC used to have high limits and bank LMN also use to sanction project-specific limits in the form of Working Capital Demand Loans (WCDL) for a short duration of 3-4 months. On one occasion, bank sanctioned project specific WCDL without WC margin and hence was never tracked for DP and further this WCDL was *continued for next 1 year as a regular facility without related to any specific project*. During one of the audits this fact surfaced and the client was asked to reduce the DP with immediate effect. This lead to drop in WCDL limits of the client and overdue surfacing in the account which lead to account reported as SMA2. Luckily client paid WCDL before account turning NPA.

Case – This case is related to a paper trader PQR who was banking with bank XYZ from last 7 years. During one of the Stock Audit, auditors commented about shortfall in drawing power in the account however same was missed as an observation and the account continued as such with same sanctioned limits. During audit, auditors raised observation that account was allowed to operate beyond drawing power for more than 6 months though there were negative comments from Stock Auditor. Issue was raised with PQR who told that he was ignorant of the fact as nobody raised it earlier. In fact, he provided supportive documents to show that there was DP. However, Stock Audit Report mentioned about denial of PQR providing supportive documents at the time of audit leading them to put remarks on the shortage of DP in the report. Though the bank got all validations later on from client and tried to convince the Auditors but all efforts went into vain and the bank had to drop DP. PQR also expressed its inability in bringing down the account within DP with such short notice leading account turning as substandard.

Learning – *We need to be very specific in terms of observations raised in audits and need to ensure timely action and imbibe learnings from same.*

Let us now see the example which is indicative of losses bank would have suffered due to non-familiarity to basic compliance requirement.

CASE – In one of the instances, bank A took over the account from another financial institution and provided both working capital and LAP loan to the client. There was an existing LAP loan which was to be taken over by the bank with a higher amount and longer tenor than what it was with the existing institution. Compliance gave green signal to go through as the LAP account was running satisfactorily and there were no overdue and the period was being increased looking to incremental amount provided under LAP. The account was going well with good cash flows and no overdue in the account.

On next renewal client asked for additional LAP amount and looking to its satisfactory conduct and sufficient repayment capability, team proposed incremental amount in the existing LAP along with extension in repayment period so as to keep the EMI at same level. During the course of a sanction one of the sanctioning authority raised apprehension about extending tenor of existing loan with bank. According to him this could lead to restructuring of account.

Since, team has already done this structure one year back they put up their argument in support of this action basis same step taken last time at the time of takeover of the account. They were right in their thought basis already done deal in the past. However, what they missed here was – In earlier transaction they have taken over LAP from other institution and have provided top up on it and hence increment in tenor was right and will not fall under purview of restructuring. In the current situation, the term loan line was in the bank's book only and the proposition was to enhance tenor of that loan which could be construed as restructuring.

The team obtained the views of the compliance department, which was also in sync with what sanctioning authority advised. Compliance view was – Any modification in tenor or EMI (reduction) in existing loan will lead to restructuring. Finally, the team proposed a second, new line of LAP loan in addition to the existing one and closed the sanction.

There was a clear Learning – *Employees should be aware of basic regulatory and internal policies and in case there is doubt, it should be referred to compliance or policy department to have their guidance on the matter.*

It is also important to study the trends of breaches on processes whether it pertains to a particular geography, particular customers and also to a particular employee. There can be a breach on one occasion but it cannot be repetitive. Even occurrence at first instance (irrespective of amount) needs to be handled seriously and message needs to be passed to the concerned person. Even after this, if there is a repeated pattern, it indicates towards something which we can be termed as **"Intentional."** This may be a scenario where somebody is trying to test the system and is waiting to do something quite big and substantial. Analysis for the trends of frauds in the banking system can second it.

Not only breaches regarding adherence to processes but also the pattern of logins, rejections and withdrawal of credit proposals need to be closely watched:

1. High rejections and withdrawals from particular geography or person-specific – Due to adverse performance and financial reasons

2. High rejections and withdrawals from particular geography or person specific – Due to adverse dedupe reporting

For the above two scenarios, we need to sit with the team and understand the sourcing and guide them accordingly. If any trend is visible, the same needs to be reported to seniors to take appropriate steps.

1. Login under one particular industry domain from specific geography (Not all as it is normal if that is the dominant industry in that particular geography)

2. Majority of logged in cases from the particular location has the same Auditor.

Additionally, as a person in asset banking domain, we should be well versed with all the Red Flag Parameters (RFA) and be always vigilant in respect of activities in the account which raises a red flag. RBI has circulated a list of some Early Warning Signals (EWS) which should alert the bank officials about some wrongdoings in the loan accounts which may turn out to be fraudulent (See Annex-I to the chapter)

Following figure, A clearly depict the areas and actionable of a person responsible for asset business in the bank. There may be some other areas which can be part of this framework. Nevertheless, these five goalkeepers provide extensive coverage to ensure right compliance ethos.

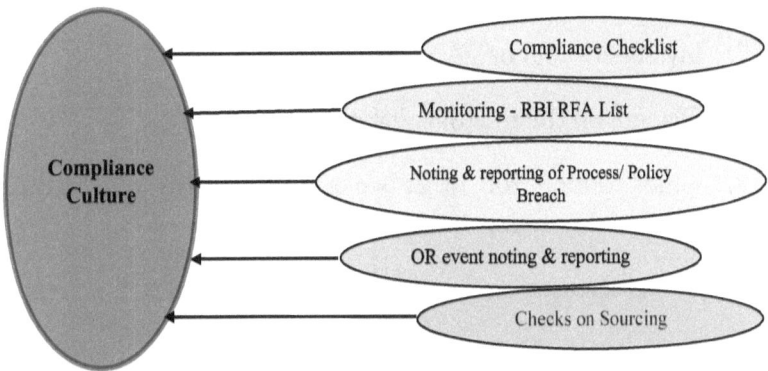

Compliance Goal Keepers

Lastly, would suggest that all of us should analyse the past cases classified as fraud by our own institution as well as frauds transpired in the industry. Also, discussions with and formal trainings by Compliance teams and Risk Containment Units plays a very important role in our preparedness to identify and avert the breach in the security of our system

Annexure – I (To Chapter 6)

1. a) Default in undisputed payment to the statutory bodies as declared in the Annual report.

    b) Bouncing of high-value cheques

2. Frequent change in the scope of the project to be undertaken by the borrower

3. Foreign bills remaining outstanding with the bank for a long time and tendency for bills to remain overdue.

4. Delay observed in payment of outstanding dues.

5. Frequent invocation of BGs and devolvement of LCs.

6. Underinsured or over-insured inventory.

7. Invoices devoid of TAN and other details.

8. Dispute on the title of collateral securities.

9. Funds coming from other banks to liquidate the outstanding loan amount unless in the normal course.

10. In merchanting trade, import leg not revealed to the bank.

11. Request received from the borrower to postpone the inspection of the godown for flimsy reasons.

12. Funding of the interest by sanctioning additional facilities.

13. Exclusive collateral charged to a number of lenders without NOC of existing charge holders.

14. Concealment of certain vital documents like master agreement, insurance coverage.

15. Floating front/associate companies by investing borrowed money

16. Critical issues highlighted in the stock audit report.

17. Liabilities appearing in ROC search report, not reported by the borrower in its annual report

18. Frequent requests for general purpose loans.

19. Frequent ad hoc sanctions.

20. Not routing of sales proceeds through consortium I member bank/lenders to the company.

21. LCs issued for local trade I related party transactions without underlying trade transaction

22. High-value RTGS payment to unrelated parties.

23. Heavy cash withdrawal in loan accounts.

24. Non-production of original bills for verification upon request.

25. Significant movements in inventory, disproportionately differing vis-a-vis change in the turnover.

26. Significant movements in receivables, disproportionately differing vis-à-vis change in the turnover and/or increase in ageing of the receivables

27. Disproportionate change in other current assets

28. Significant increase in working capital borrowing as a percentage of turnover

29. Increase in Fixed Assets, without a corresponding increase in long term sources (when a project is implemented).

30. Increase in borrowings, despite huge cash and cash equivalents in the borrower's balance sheet

31. Frequent change in the accounting period and/or accounting policies

32. Costing of the project which is in wide variance with the standard cost of installation of the project

33. Claims not acknowledged as debt high

34. Substantial increase in unbilled revenue year after year.

35. Large number of transactions with inter-connected companies and large outstanding from such companies

36. Substantially related party transactions

37. Material discrepancies in the annual report

38. Significant inconsistencies within the annual report (between various sections)

39. Poor disclosure of materially adverse information and no qualification by the statutory auditors

40. A raid by Income tax/sales tax/central excise duty officials

41. Significant reduction in the stake of promoter/director or increase in the encumbered shares of promoter/director.

42. Resignation of the key personnel and frequent changes in the management

Chapter 7

Are We Future Ready?

All of us are well aware of below concepts and their applications. These are becoming backbone of normal banking and we are imbibing them in our daily routine.

Digitization	Automation	Artificial Intelligence
Machine Learning	Block Chain	Data Analytics
Mobile Banking	Anywhere Anytime Banking	
Score Card based Analysis		Auto Processing

Time is changing. And it is changing fast. Along with it, the way we work is also changing. When I started my career in banking twenty-two years back, we all use to make our memo by hand or use to get it typed by the stenographers. This was the time when the officials in branches use to make FDs and update passbooks by hand. All this changed with banks adopting computerization. We all started making credit proposals on computers and used to sign after taking printouts. This has also changed now and all the things now happen on digital platforms with a seamless transition of information from one end to other and all approvals in digital modes.

Above is the scenario till date, which all of my young readers are now well attuned to. They have already started experiencing Automation and AI (Artificial Intelligence). Usage of AI in credit underwriting and monitoring is at the initial stage as on date, and with the passage of time, it will make deeper inroads. However, Automation in credit underwriting has already entered into a big way though restricted to consumer, micro and small loans as of now. Automation is enabling faster turnaround time and improved customer interface.

Overall, Banking/FIs domain is observing structural shift driven by following three broad parameters:

> **Incremental Customer expectations** – Customer expectations are being driven by extensive use of technology and is becoming norm for the customers.

> **Tightened regulations and compliance** – Increased occurrences of frauds, money laundering, terrorist finances etc have led to stricter compliance framework in place by the regulators

> **Heightened competition** – Banks and NBFCs are facing challenges from FinTech who have brought in a great amount of innovation in the segment

To handle above, banks need to provide rapid, real-time answers, customized products and services, and instant decisions to the customers. They need to put in strong compliance and monitoring framework and build compliance adherence culture in an organisation. It requires process overhauling and the use of non-traditional data (prepopulated data from public and govt sources) to take decisions. Banks and NBFC are doing but have to do more on data analytics and use of AI to remain in the race.

Now the big question is (Q)–Whether more and more automation of underwriting and monitoring will bring redundancy to the credit manager's job?

Pause: Will request the reader to close her/his eyes and think whether it is possible? Note down your thoughts on plain paper. Close it now and open it only once you are through this chapter.

We shall converse on the following three concepts here and will keep our discussion intertwined around them:

1. Adaptability Quotient

2. Learning Inquisitiveness

3. Design thinking

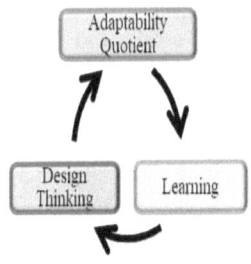

Fig A

ADAPTABILITY

AQ is an ability to adapt and thrive in an environment of change

"It is not the strongest of the species that survives, nor the most intelligent. It is the one that is most adaptable to change" – ***Charles Darwin***

"Nobody likes to change. There will always be resistant to change, and there always will be change. And the quicker you get to that, the easier it is. It's not such a difficult thing. If you entrench yourself and go, 'By God, I will not change, I will not have this.' Then, you're a dead man. We're great at adaptability. It's our strongest suit" – Nick Nolte

"All failure is failure to adapt, all success is successful adaptation" – ***Max McKeown***

LEARNING

Inquisitiveness makes learning more effective and enjoyable

"Anyone who stops learning is old. Whether at twenty or Eighty" – ***Henry Ford***

"Live as if you were to die tomorrow. Learn as if you were to live forever" – Mahatma Gandhi

"Once you stop learning, you start dying" – ***Albert Einstein***

DESIGN THINKING

Design thinking process seeks to understand people's requirements and find the effective solutions to meet those requirements

"Design thinking is a human-centred approach to innovation that draws from the designer's toolkit to integrate the needs of people, the possibilities of technology, and the requirements for business success" – **Tim Brown**

"Creativity is a mindset, a way of thinking and a proactive approach to finding new solutions. We may not all be artists, but we can be more creative professionals" – Extract from book 'Creative Confidence' by Tom Kelley & David Kelley

"Design thinking is neither art nor science nor religion. It is the capacity, ultimately, for integrative thinking" – **Tim Brown**

"We can't solve problems by using the same kind of thinking we used when we created them" – Albert Einstein

---

Let us go through three different case studies touching these three concepts. Hope they will further take us nearer to the resolution of apprehension raised in question (Q) at the start of the chapter.

CASE (Adaptability): Bank PQR launched a Scorecard based loan sanctioning process. There were different grades (A, B, C) which decides whether the case shall be Straight Pass or will require some subjective analysis also. Also, security coverage was linked to different grades. This was an effort in the direction of minimizing subjective analysis up to certain loan amounts. Which, in turn, will improve the overall turnaround time (TAT) and productivity. Trainings were held to make people aware of the product and the purpose of the same.

In the first six months of launch, total sanctions under category 'A' (which was straight pass-through) were quite low vis a vis desired numbers. Additionally, TAT under category 'A' was higher than what was targeted for. Meetings were held with the first and second line of managers to understand the issues being faced by them. The conversations lead to the conclusion that members have apprehensions in allowing cases to straight pass through. According to them, there were some factors in every deal which they feel may bring the credit down and hence they shifted it to other grades of B and C for taking higher securities or they asked for additional information which leads to higher TAT.

Seniors addressed their apprehension and conveyed following to them:

1. There are defined **Go-No-Go parameters** based on dedupes and some of the critical financial parameters. The proposal shall be rejected at this stage itself if it does not pass Go-No-Go parameters.

2. It is a scorecard based underwriting and different weightages have already been provided for several pertinent factors based on their significance in the overall sanction process

3. Within each parameter, there are '4' options of providing marks from 1 to 4. So, the scorecard itself is taking care of the analyst's view once marks are assigned accordingly.

   For example, in a particular case if the analyst has apprehension about high Leverage, then the case will be outrightly rejected if leverage is higher than hurdle rate set for the program in Go No Go Parameters. If leverage is lower than the set hurdle rates but still is seemingly higher than what an analyst expect, then there is a grid for providing marks within that parameter and analyst can assign marks on a spectrum of 1 to 4.

   Important to understand is that that scorecard gives results after cumulative scores of all the factors. *One factor cannot influence the scores.*

4. Different weightages and deflators are crystallized upon after doing back testing on available sample cases of last seven to ten years.

After addressing the apprehensions there was some improvement but it took further rounds of mentoring and further three to four months for things to get streamlined.

Above is a perfect example on **"Adaptability."** Since, employees were *too used to subjective* analysis, *they were hesitant in adopting new process with Nil or very Low subjective underwriting*

Now there is a twist going forward in this Scorecard Story – Seniors called for MIS after twelve months of launch so as to carry review. Results were eye opener for all. There was a substantial improvement in overall approval and TAT under the category 'A'. The other thing which was even more eye-catching was—*out of overall modifications done in Scorecard and the process itself, eighty-five percent were suggested by the ground team members.*

Three things learnt from above behaviour of team are:

1. **Ignorance** – Ignorance is the biggest hurdle on our way to Adaptability. Our acceptance or rejection of any new concept, process or product should be done post our complete understanding of it

2. **Unlearning** – Sometimes to learn new things in life, we have to follow the process of unlearning old things which may have less relevance in the present environment

3. **Mentoring** – Pre-launch mentoring on a new product, policy, concept, process through discussions, trainings and con-calls will improve the adaptability quotient of team

CASE (Learning): Seniors were sitting with their team to evaluate the portfolio position for a particular period. They were doing the review on account by account basis for understanding the business, slippages, recovery etc. During the discussion they observed that team was well aware of their accounts and portfolio. Team members were hands-on about the portfolio.

During the course of review, seniors switched discussion from portfolio towards present trend of banking. Seniors started inquiring on the subject to check knowledge levels of a team about the latest happening in the banking. Statistics was not encouraging – Only 30% of the team members were well aware about new technological trends, AI applications being used by the industry members; 50% of members have heard about all the concepts mentioned but does not have entrenched understanding; 20% of the members were aware only about part of the mentioned concepts.

Seniors asked team to go through the latest happenings in the field of technology and analytics and also asked 30% of participants (who were well aware of these new developments) to do mentoring on this side of banking. They also asked regional teams to conduct fortnightly sessions at their locations to discuss on the latest trends in banking. In addition to that, the team also use to share their experiences and learnings from portfolio pertaining to underwriting, monitoring, trade-related activities etc. In fact, in many sessions, young team members use to discuss matters which introduce senior members to newer concepts which they were not aware of.

The learning from above are:

1. **Learning is an on-going process** – We all need to be aware of the latest happening around us. For this, we need to be a keen reader and listener.

2. **Learning is both way** – It can be from the topmost in the hierarchy to the lowest one and vice-versa. Important for all of us is to be continually in search of gaining knowledge

3. **Learn from Other's experiences** – Why to wait to learn from our mistakes? Learn from others mistakes so as to prevent our self from even committing a mistake in a first stance. Similarly, take a cue from good experiences of others so that we can save our time on iteration in doing any work

CASE (Design Thinking):

Group of underwriters were given a job to come out with a program for funding in a particular trade domain on the principals of:

1. Minimum TAT (turnaround time)

2. Collecting Optimum information to take a decision

3. Maximum due diligence

So, the challenge for the team was to:

– Give product which provides decision basis lesser information than what was being used till date

– Should take lesser end to end time from file pick-up to disbursement than what was being taken till now

– Over this, they were asked not to compromise with due diligence which should remain watertight

Group of analysts sit together and after a week of discussion between themselves, they come out with a product which, according to them, was in line with the guidance provided.

Without going into a discussion on product, the manager asked them to do the following:

a. Present the product to a limited group of their colleagues from relationship at a regional level

b. Present the product to a limited group of their colleagues from the underwriting team at a regional level

c. Note down their feedback and present

d. To be done within the next three days

After three days, team members came back to the manager and asked for an extension of two days. He smiled and gave them two more days. Once again, after the passage of two days, they again came to the manager and asked for a further two days. He again smiled and gave them an additional three days but conveyed them that this is the final extension.

After three days when the team came back to the manager, he asked them why it took them too long in collecting feedback. They narrated that during the feedback session with the team on the ground they realized that initially, they had not included many of the things required for execution at ground zero. Hence, basis these feedbacks they did modifications in the product, which took time.

The manager went through the presentation and provided his suggestions and also asked team to run pass it through some of the existing good customers to take their feedback. Post inclusion of manager's suggestions and feedback from the customers, team could develop product that was not only in line with the conveyed guidelines but was a first of its type in the industry.

The learnings which flows from the above case are:

1. **Understand the problem first** – For this take feedbacks of actual users and record them as Problem Statements

2. **Try to find out solutions to these Problem statements** – Set of these solutions will be the base for your product

3. **Test your product for further feedbacks** – Be ready for round of iterations

4. **Apply suggestions and finalize product** – which is in sync with requirements of ground team and the customers as they are the ultimate user and beneficiary. Their non acceptance will prove nonstarter for the product devised.

Adaptability is the first stage of change however it is not the only thing which can make transformation smooth. It needs to be followed by learning, inquisitiveness and desire to give something new, something different. And the process to do something different should be structured in line with Design Thinking process so that modifications or changes matches end-user expectations. *Important also is to understand that these three concepts are not static or one-time activity but are to be imbibed as a habit and to be practiced regularly.*

In all the above three situations have you noticed one thing which is common to all. Who all were involved in the process of *developing* new product, *application* of new concepts, *implementation* of new products? Answer is – "**You.**" In all the new products, processes and policies developed and modified till date, there will always be a major contribution of people who are the domain experts. We cannot conceptualize anything without having basics clear about the activity. Can anybody without knowledge of banking and credit develop automated credit decision-making systems, Loan Origination System (LOS), Loan Monitoring Systems (LMS)? The **answer is "No."**

Have we ever asked ourselves that what is our design thinking quotient? Can we suggest something new to the industry which can be better for clients than existing products (ease of understanding, cheaper, enhanced accessibility, agility). Our endeavour to do something new or bringing some modified version of what we are doing will increase our inquisitiveness and thus our **"Design Thinking Quotient"**.

Why we cannot find new way of doing underwriting, new processes or new products? This will require exploitation of existing processes and products available so as have outcome which is better than the existing products and processes. We need to regularly question ourselves and our stakeholders including clients to understand their problem statements and what they expect from the bank/FI we are working in.

In fact, regular discussion with new employees or trainees, who have yet to get infested by an existing environment of an organisation, can provide us with insights which can be very new or unheard of. On the lines of Design Thinking, we have to experiment and iterate a lot to arrive at a workable, feasible and optimal solution or product. Have we thought of how we shall be able to survive when there are new generation entities bringing niche products in the market with the support of available data bank and the digital platforms available?

In my banking career, I have not seen much of new development on product and process side which may provide the customer a different experiment. Yes, the big change I observed in these years is the way manual operations getting automated to improve the efficiency and productivity. Along with this, customer service has improved through digital interface, enabling the customer to do transactions on the move and 24*7 service availability. However, in terms of products available to the customer, the spread is quite limited. *From the time I entered into banking domain to till date I have seen limited asset products like Cash*

Credit, Overdraft, Bill purchase, Term Loans etc. being offered to different customers in different sizes and tenors with a topping of suitable pricings and margins with agreed security coverage. This is the area where we can work and come out with new products with support of our IT and Analytics team members

Newer concepts of Information Technology & Data Analytics are enablers and are there to make our jobs easier and faster. It is good for us to understand this as soon as possible and adapt the same fast. Our openness and acceptance of all the changes which are happening around will lead to a healthier team work for providing something new and fresh to the industry.

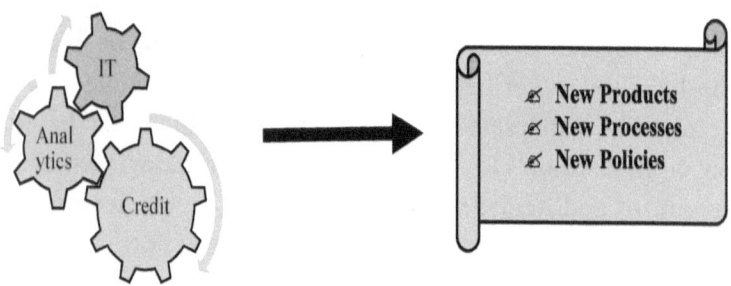

I hope that you have the answer to your question Q. As Stephen Covey has described in his book – "Seven Habits of highly effective people" that 'principals' are permanent while 'values' may change as demands or needs change. Similarly, role of credit in overall scheme of things in banking will remain as important as it is today. It will never be redundant but yes there will be a modification in the overall delivery mechanism.

One fact which all of us have to acknowledge is – *Roles will not become redundant but we shall become redundant if we do not improve our "Adaptability Quotient", do not "Keep on Learning" and do not "think as a Designer."*

Chapter 8

Credit Manager – As I Would like to Be

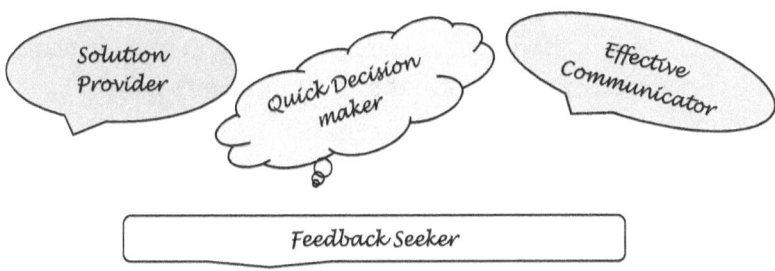

Our qualification and level of domain expertise can act as an enabler for us to get our job. However, the way we exhibit, demonstrate, share our knowledge and empathize with people around us decide course of our journey in an organisation.

Till now we talked about the technical aspects of skill sets required by a credit manager and what shall be the trend going forward.

We shall now be discussing about the soft skills and behavioural aspects which are required to be part of a personality. Direction and degree of these traits add to define our persona and their mix vary from person to person.

Sometimes, direction (+ or -), degree and mix of these traits get shaped up by our work profile. However, here we shall keep our discussion limited to an individual in the role of credit managers basis what I have understood from my experience in the role.

Person A can be more knowledgeable than person B but person B can be more successful as a credit manager because B has better communication skills. Similarly, person C can be successful than both A and B if C has an optimum mix of all the qualities which A and B together have. Let us start our discussion to understand the importance of each trait in the credit manager's profile:

Trait I (Solution Provider) – What can be the right thing which can happen in our life. Probably, obtaining "Solution" to every problem we face in life — "Yes." But the best situation will be wherein we have friends around who are not only capable of solving our problems but also take steps to create an environment with minimal problems. We call these friends "Solution Providers."

They are the people who:

1. Welcome colleagues with smiling faces and are forever ready to listen them with open mind

2. Are proactive in identifying the problem and providing a solution

3. Work to correct and streamline the whole process to remove the hurdles

4. Their optimism Index is quite high and hence they start the search for a solution on a positive note

Why should we wait for somebody to approach us with a problem to get a solution? It is better that we should extend our hand for assistance first. Our problem-solving ability is linked to our readiness to understand the situation and eagerness to help others.

More than our subject knowledge, it is our attitude that creates a difference.

Problem-solving is both an Art and Science. Art, as it requires unperturbed temperament to handle the situation and Science as it requires the application of permutation and combination to look for the "optimal" solution. The whole process of Problem-Solving and Solution-Finding can be like:

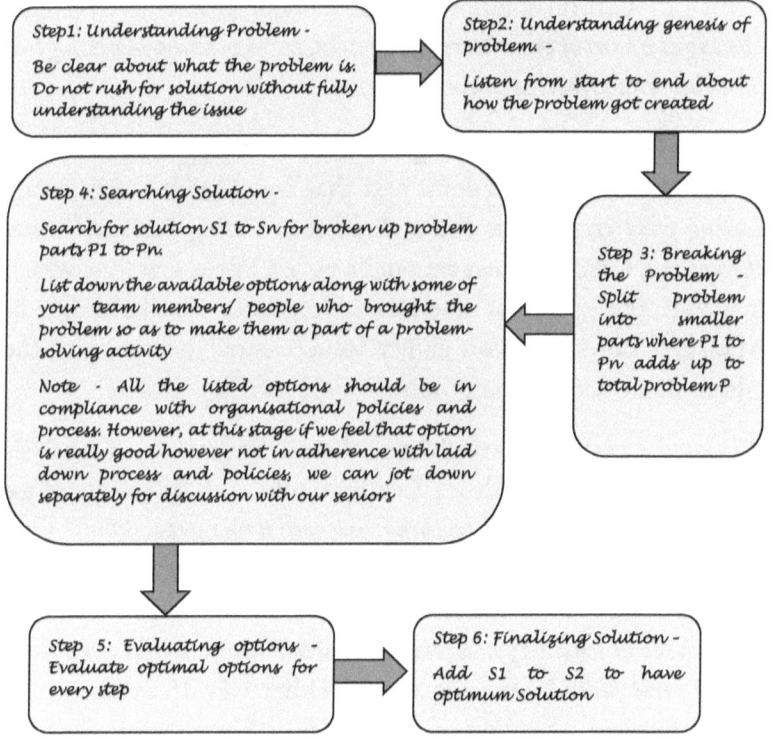

Have observed three obstacles in our "Problem Solving Ability." **First one** is our rush to provide opinion without understanding the whole matter. Einstein has said *"If I had an hour to solve a problem, I'd spend 55 minutes thinking about the problem and 5 minutes thinking about solution."* **Second one** is our attitude of

"Me First" which defeat the very purpose of exploring solution through Combined Wisdom of a Team. And the **Third one** is *"One size fit all"* approach which confines our thoughts and hence lead to sub optimal solution with longer than desired time.

I got a message on my WhatsApp—very apt and connected with our discussion. It reads like – A door is much smaller compared to the house. A lock is much smaller compared to the door and key is the smallest of all, but a key can open entire house. Thus, a small thoughtful solution can solve major problems. *Problem-solving is a sum of our enterprising zeal, team management, logical thinking and effective communication.*

Trait II (Quick Decisioning) – In my training sessions I have always stressed on one point and that is – Quick Decisioning. *Losing good credit is as bad a decision as letting bad credit into the system.* Credit Managers ought to act like a Catalyst which increases the speed of a chemical reaction. Similarly, Credit Managers quick decision ability to accelerate the speed of the whole client-acquisition process.

As a credit analyst, I have always believed that too much Analysis leads to paralysis. As Bruce Lee has aptly said *"If you spend too much time thinking about a thing, you will never get it done"* What it implies that spending too much time on a particular matter or proposition does not lead anywhere. Someone has said that *"Think too much and you'll create a problem that was not even there in the first place."* Decision can be either way. It can be either an approval or a decline of a proposal or a transaction, but the essence should be to do it fast.

In today's banking world, customer's priority is Faster Service Delivery Time and to fulfil that, all the people in service delivery chain need to ensure fast decisions. As a Credit Manager, we are responsible for one of the most important leg of asset acquisition and relationship process i.e. sanction process. For a customer it is not pertinent that which department takes how much time. Customer is dealing with a bank/NBFC and for its what matters is end to end time from submission of documents to stage it receives money in the account. Customer is concerned with end to end turnaround time (ETAT). Many a time we lose good clients to competition due to longer decision-making time.

Besides losing good clients due to slow decision-making, we sometimes miss on vital facts to be analysed and also run risk of giving entry to a bad account into the system. As a practice customer puts his credit request with 2-3 banks/FIs simultaneously. This creates a situation of intense competition in the market space. The moment the customer brings the sanction from another institution, we hurriedly close half-baked proposals due to fear of losing the client. This partial analysis sometimes leads to the missing out of vital credit facts which can have adverse consequences going ahead.

There are occasions when we are in a dilemma about what is right or wrong and hence not able to take a decision on our own. This stage requires us to consult our team leaders, explain the case, transaction or situation, put up our views and finally obtain their views on it. This enable to move the things faster. However, do not make it a practice. This situation should not be more than 10-20% of our total assignments handled in a particular period. If we make it a regular feature then certainly, we are going to lose our relevance in the system, making us dependent on our seniors for anything we do. Psychologically also it makes us weak and people start skipping us and start approaching our seniors. One thing I would like to highlight here is that whenever we are taking a matter for discussion with our seniors, we have to necessarily put up our views and points before concluding the decision.

Sometimes, inducement of the gut is so strong that we take the decision without having the right analytics and objectivity around our decision. We must always avoid our gut feel to come in play at the time of taking the decision. Similarly, our decision ought not be influenced by our good or bad perception about the person who has brought the case or transaction for approval. This distracts us from analysing the strength and weaknesses of the case or transaction as our decision shall be basis our bias or detestation towards the person. The third behavioural aspect which affects our decision is our own "Ego." Our ego obstructs our listening ability and understanding others point of view. It restricts our capacity to take right downloads from others, thus leading to one-sided decision which may be as per our satisfaction but lack general consensus.

Quick decision-making does not always implies that we have to provide decision as soon as we receive case or transaction to approve. The pace of decision-making has direct correlation with available information related to the case. There is always a least amount of information which is required to take a decision and we have to wait for availability of this information (quantum varies from task to task). Many a time I have come across the situation where immediately after finishing our meeting with client, relationship manager ask about my decision. As a practice I never give my decision immediately after meeting client and take another 3-4 hours to a days' time for the same. Reason for same shall be clear basis steps explained below:

Step 1: Go through the information provided at the time of initial login

Step 2: Discuss with client to understand its business model and points on which further clarity required

Step 3: Come back to your workplace. Assimilate already available information with downloads from meeting with the client. Then take a final decision

This is required as sometimes client provide information at the time of the meeting which is missing in the initial login of case. Our interpretation of case gets revised with clarification/additional information available from the client

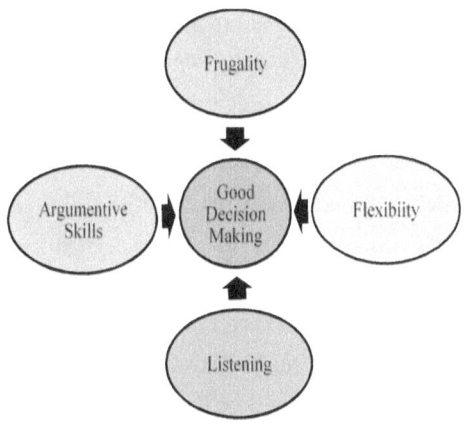

Decisioning Essentials

As described above, a good decision requires:

1. **Frugality** – Taking credit decision with minimal information is what differentiates us from others. Any credit proposal requires not more than 4-5 factors to have a fair idea to whether proceed ahead or reject it. Once we are convinced to go ahead, we can do elaborative assessment and structuring of the proposal in hand. These 4-5 factors are very critical and have a deep impact on credit quality. If we are able to identify these factors and do a quick analysis around them to do Probability (of occurrence) and Impact assessment, our key job is done

2. **Flexibility** – We need to be flexible in our approach. Flexible to understand others point of view and to understand that the present situation may be different from situations in which we have taken earlier credit decisions. Accordingly, we can modify our approach. Flexibility also refers to our ability to modify our decisions on the basis of new facts presented or information received in due course of the decision-making process

3. **Listening** – Listen to what others have to say before giving the decision. If we do not listen to others, we run a risk of giving decision basis half of the facts available. Listening to others also increase acceptability of our decision

4. **Argumentive Skills** – This is one of the skill sets which are core to Credit Manager's role. Arguments are always correlated with loud and aggressive discussions, which is entirely incorrect. Healthy arguments between Credit and Relationship team are always welcomed and lead to opening up of new horizon and broaden the thought process. Collins dictionary states that *"An **argument** is a statement or set of statements that you use in order to try to convince people that your opinion about something is correct."* Decision without arguments between the two teams suggests that either of the team is not disposing of its responsibility well. Hence, arguments are an integral part of the decision process. It is important to control our emotions, be prepared with our facts and figures and keep our egos in check while arguing on the subject

Trait III (Effective Communication): How often do we communicate with our seniors, colleagues, stakeholders, subordinate? How effective is our communication? Do we require any modification in our approach? Have we ever analysed this?

Oxford dictionary says that "communication is the activity or process of expressing **ideas** and **feelings** or of giving people information."

Collins dictionary says that "communication is the act or an instance of communicating; the imparting exchange of information, **ideas** or **feelings**."

Macmillan dictionary says that "communication is the process of giving information or of making **emotions** or **ideas** known to someone"

*See the highlighted words and sentences in all the definitions – **All speak about the exchange of ideas and expression of emotions and feelings***

Now see what our great personalities and laureates have to say:

Peter Drucker – "The most important thing in communication is **hearing what isn't said**"

Zig Ziglar – "In many ways, effective communication begins with **mutual respect**, communication that **inspires, encourages** others to do their best"

John C. Maxwell – "People may hear your words, but they **feel** your **attitude**"

All the quotes above emphasize on feelings, respect, inspiration, encouragement similar to what dictionary definitions are. Think about a person in your organization whom all others adore. I am sure that one of the qualities for which all shall be admiring that person will be his/her **effective way of communication.** As Jim Rohn has said **"If you just communicate, you can get by. But if you communicate skilfully, you can work miracles."**

Communication can be a verbal, non-verbal or written one and for them to be effective, it requires these 7 C's:

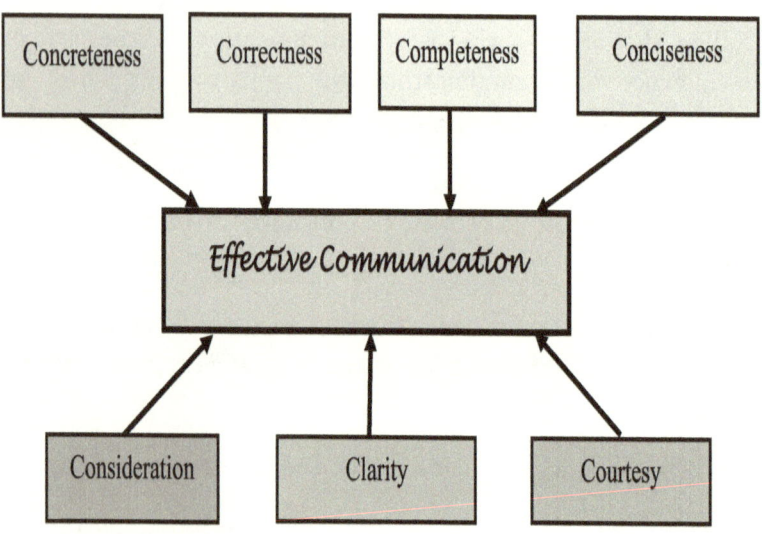

Let us visualize our daily interaction with office colleagues. Are we doing it in the same fashion as what is explained above? Do a small exercise—benchmark your way of communicating with all the 7C's. This will aid you in ascertaining your area of improvement.

Though all the factors are important for effective message however if I have to list down these 7 C's in order of their weightage, I shall consider lower 3Cs as base and keep them in priority group No1 while other 4 C's in priority group No 2. Let us see what the bottom 3 C's means and what is their importance in a Credit Role:

Consideration – Do we talk or write a message with receiver in mind? If not, then this need to be changed. This is what is element "Consideration" in our communication is. It is like "stepping into the shoes of others." Give consideration to receiver's viewpoints, their requirements, problems, emotions, attitude, desires. It is important to empathize with the receiver which shall inspire them to indulge in positive communication with us.

Courtesy – Every action has its reaction. Similarly, we get what we give or what we convey through our communication, whether it is verbal or written. Receptiveness and revert to our message by the receiver are directly proportional to the level of courtesy we show. Our message is reflective of our expression and hence should be polite and judicious in tone. It is not necessary that our tone of message (whether verbal or written) be harsher if we want to convey our displeasure. The tone of our message under all the circumstances need to positive and focused.

Clarity – What will be our reaction to the talk or message which is complex and not to the mark? We surely will try to close the discussion fast and in case of the mail message, will keep it in abeyance or will direct it to the *"delete folder"*. Complexity in the content and messages suppresses good communications. The message should be easy to comprehend and straight without being unpleasant

Do make modifications in your communication in line with what we discussed above and you will surely observe positive changes in overall working environment around you. I am quoting some of the instances here to substantiate what we discussed.

One of my young colleagues approached me and complained that he does not get the reverts on time or get incomplete revert and this is a regular feature. This results in an elongated, end-to-end TAT (ETAT). He also informed that this is an issue with most of the relationship individuals. I went through a sample of queries raised by him and suggested him some modification in the style of putting queries and ask him to come back to me after a months' time. After one month, we both sat together and went through the TAT tracker. There was a substantial improvement in ETAT. He informed me that it was a result of the suggested modification in the technique of putting and resolving the query. I am jotting down those suggestions here:

1. **Change the tone of the mail from commanding to suggestive and support it with reasons for asking (Please note that nobody is going to take anybody's ego)**

   Scenario 1: Provide ABC information from the client

   Scenario 2: Please collect ABC information from client as it is required for analysing particular point

2. **Highlight that both of you are a part of team and working for the same cause**

   Scenario 1: Correct the spreads

   Scenario 2: Please rectify the spreads as they are not yielding correct picture of business. In case of any difficulty please come to me, I will guide you on the same

3. **Clarity on what we want by subdividing queries**

   Scenario 1: All the queries from serial number 1 to 10

   Scenario 2: Part A – Queries 1 to 4 on information required from client

   Part B – Queries 5 to 8 on correction required in proposal

   Part C – Queries 9 to 10 on incomplete details to be filled

4. Pick up the phone and talk to relationship person about all these query points and then put mail for record purpose

All the above suggestions are what I have followed in my earlier days as a Credit Manager and have seen yielding very good results. More than the improvement in TAT, this also helps to have a better bonding with different stakeholders. All the above suggestions take into consideration all the 7Cs and especially bottom 3Cs, which we have discussed elaborately.

The modified approach helps in removing the negative perception that sometimes creeps in between a credit and relationship person as our role requires questioning and arguments. It also takes us out of the silos as we talk face to face or on the phone to discuss matters. It is always advisable to pick up the phone and talk or if in the same office, then it became easy to sit together and resolve instead of exchanging everything on mail. Rightly said by Nat Turner that **"Good Communication is the bridge between confusion and clarity."**

Trait IV (Feedback Seeker): Our progression in life is somewhat based on the view people hold about us. And this stands equally true for all the stakeholders irrespective of whether it is our superior, peer, junior or an external stakeholder. All the traits discussed above can be modified with time and experience. *Important for us is to keep ourself open for feedback and application of learnings derived.* Sometimes, feedback provides us with the outcomes which catch us totally unaware of the same or they are contrary to our perception about ourself. More significant for us is to take feedback pointers in a positive manner and keep working on them to improve.

Feedback is not an one-time affair but is a continuous process wherein you take feedback then act on it, measure your progress and set of areas which still require to work upon. Go back to the same set of individuals to take feedback. Continue this process till you arrive at your set benchmark for a particular trait.

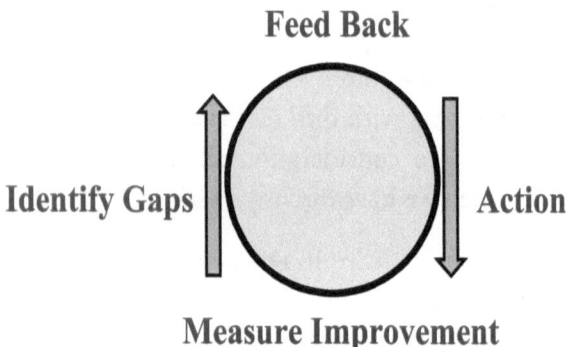

Feed Back

Identify Gaps   **Action**

Measure Improvement

Another vital point in the process is the Universe Size and spread. Our feedback needs to be spread across all the stakeholders who are part of our work biosphere – both vertically (Superiors, colleagues and subordinates) and laterally (relationship managers and colleagues from other business verticals). In most of the organisation HR department conduct 360-degree feedback reviews which can help to derive the inputs required to take action on. However, I feel that periodic informal reviews should also be part of our feedback process and it really help when we genuinely act on them.

I will also suggest that we should also need to have the temperament to accept negative feedback and patience to act upon. It is a slow corrective process as it requires unlearning of and modification in our long-imbibed thoughts along with simultaneous learning of something new which we have not ever practised.

Learning from Feedbacks on us by others is one part. *The other part of learning comes from others Feedback about somebody.* ***Process of improving ourselves should be a sum of both.*** I call this as the **"Quadrant Theory."**

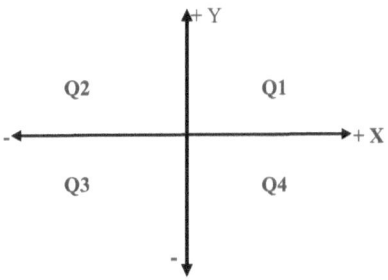

In the above diagram, X (+) is Our Strength and X (-) is Our weakness. Similarly, Y (+) is Others positive and Y (-) is Others Negative

See others positive and take download from it. This will be + for you. Also, see your strengths and use them. It will be + for you. So, now you have two + with you. Similarly, you have +, +, or you can have -, -, -. So, it is like learning from feedback about others and also learning from what others perceive about you. Like learning from + of others and yours, negative of others and weakness of yours also give you a lesson to abstain from these negative traits and also present you with an opportunity to add more +s so that you can negate the impact of negative in order to keep yourself in Q1.

Notes